Research as Social Change

Have you ever thought research is boring? 'Research', writes Umberto Eco, 'should be fun.' It seems unlikely that Umberto Eco has read many of the standard texts that are given to students in the social sciences or education to study. But boredom is only text deep, for social research offers possibilities for the exploration of ideas and for the involvement of the researcher and researched alike in projects that can be informative, sometimes revelatory and fun to do. This book, part manual and part travel guide, shows us how by turning some unexpected corners research, like teaching, can be seen as a deeply social and personal activity.

This book is dedicated to the notion that social research should become an integral part of the contemporary workplace. Its principal concern is with integrating different forms of qualitative research, action research and case study methods within the ambit of professional practice. In pursuit of the demystification of research it turns towards the investigation of memories and personal perceptions, drawings, journal writing and photographs as sources, with the aim of developing new directions and new possibilities for research that bring together theory and practice, method and message, social organisations and their clients. It is a vital source for all who are interested in doing research but who find themselves sceptical, critical or alienated from the research they encounter.

Michael Schratz teaches methodology and curriculum innovation at the University of Innsbruck and his research interests in management and leadership in the context of educational change have recently taken him to communities in Estonia, Croatia and Australia. **Rob Walker** teaches classroom research by distance education at Deakin University, his students being located in various parts of Australia and elsewhere around the Pacific rim.

Research as Social Change

New Opportunities for Qualitative Research

Michael Schratz and Rob Walker

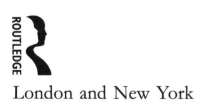

London and New York

First published 1995
by Routledge
11 New Fetter Lane, London EC4P 4EE

Simultaneously published in the USA and Canada
by Routledge
29 West 35th Street, New York, NY 10001

Typeset in Garamond by
J&L Composition Ltd, Filey, North Yorkshire
Printed and bound in Great Britain by
Biddles Ltd, Guildford and King's Lynn

British Library Cataloguing in Publication Data
A catalogue record for this book is available from the British Library

Library of Congress Cataloguing in Publication Data
A catalogue record for this book has been requested

ISBN 0–415–11868–9 (hbk)
ISBN 0–415–11869–7 (pbk)

Contents

Illustrations

FIGURES

Acknowledgements

We want to thank the many colleagues and students, who contributed in different ways to this book; some provided detailed and invaluable comments on an earlier draft, some contributed their own work and some provided encouragement at moments when our confidence in ourselves dipped. In particular our thanks go to Jürgen Störk, András Tapolcai, Onoriode Oghenekaro, Kate Seabourne, Steve Wilkinson, Bridget Somekh, Chris Bigum, Ruth Epstein, Boonda Kearns, Marie Brennan, Jack Sanger, Helen Modra, Colin Henry, Lindsay Fitzclarence, Louise Wilson, Orlando Fals-Borda, Susan Groundwater-Smith, Ann Collins, Barbara Kamler, Barbara Schratz-Hadwich, Janine Wiedel, Frigga Haug, Herbert Altrichter, Margaret Clark, Jennifer Nias, 'Justine', 'Sally', 'Jane' and 'Mark'. The 'Understandascope' (p. 73) is reproduced by courtesy of Michael Leunig. Our thanks go to Ray Walshe for the elephant pictures scattered throughout Chapter 1.

We would like to thank the three institutions where we were both faculty members during the period in which this book was written – Deakin University, the University of Innsbruck and the Centre for Peace Studies in Burgschlaining – for their support – academic, administrative, technical, collegial and financial. Rob Walker would also like to thank the Academic Development Centre at the University of the Western Cape, South Africa for their help during the final phase of completing this book.

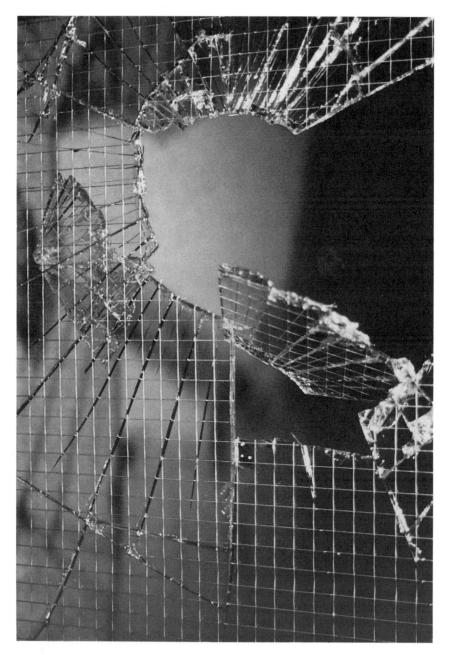

Illustration 1 'Breaking in'

'Breaking in'

Breaking through security glass into a book is an unusual way to start. Perhaps we should have rolled out a carpet for you. Either way, words and pictures are all we have, even though we have learnt from the various seminars we have given in Austria and Australia, and places between (both east and west), that in themselves they are not enough. We believe that getting involved in research is a total human experience for *everybody involved*, though the nature and intensity of this involvement is usually left out in the reports we read, even those that declare themselves to be qualitative studies. In almost all that we read about research a dimension seems to be missing, and this is reflected especially in books about research methods. So, our aim in this book is to write about *doing* research in ways that go beyond describing different methods that can be used to collect data and the uses that can be made of them in different settings and to recognise the essentially social and personal nature of research.

Illustration 1, 'Breaking in', signifies new meanings and new possibilities. The broken pane of security glass in the photograph has a history that is significant in relation to our purpose. It was part of a door in the corridor of a university building and was broken by a woman who, angry at her failure to communicate her feminist position among her male colleagues, ran from the room, slamming the door so as to keep the 'other' world behind her. The closed door, now broken, suddenly signifies new meanings and new possibilities. The department now has an influential women's studies section whose work has influenced this book. A breakthrough?

1 Social research as social action

This book is written for those who see their involvement in research providing them with new possibilities for action. For some this means finding new ways of looking at what is familiar in order to change it, for others it may begin as a need for a better understanding of changes forced on the situations in which they find themselves. For many people it means finding ways to seize the opportunity to become more reflexive in their practice, that is to say creating the means for looking at the situations in which they act as others in the situation see them.

This is intended to be a book for research beginners, but 'beginners' is a somewhat ambiguous term because in qualitiative research, perhaps more than in any other kind of research, we are all beginners every time we start a new project, and our past experience is not always as useful as we hope it will be. Nevertheless, we expect the book to be used mainly by students who are doing research as part of master's degrees or PhDs and some of the topics we have addressed have such students especially in mind. While the ideas in the book derive from our experience in educational research and evaluation, we believe it will be useful to a wide range of studies in the social sciences, in the professions and projects in those areas of applied and environmental science that touch on social conditions and consequences.

We expect our readers will come to this book with different professional and other backgrounds but that you will share the desire to search for ways of incorporating a research dimension within your particular areas of interest and concern. Consequently this book will focus on practical ways of using research as a means of improving your ability to read situations, to evaluate and extend your practice, as a way of making the bureaucracies within which you may work more responsive to client, student and staff needs and as a means of developing an educative approach to the design, delivery and assessment of training. Already it will be apparent that our view of 'research' is broad rather than specialised. It is a view that disrupts the assumption that theory and practice can be kept separate and it assumes not just that the motivations for, commitment to and practice of research

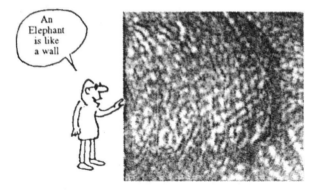

are central to the research enter-prise, but that they are inextricably as much personal as they are scientific.

Our interest is primarily with research in the context of social action rather than with research as a specialised form of academic work, but in practice this is a distinction that is becoming more and more difficult to maintain in most fields of social research, other than as a rhetorical device. The result is a confusion of the academic and the practical that is disturbing for those who see scientific method defined by a complete separation of the normative from the positive but it is a confusion we find helpful and which we will seek to extend and encourage! For conventionally, research assumes that rationality in the social situations it studies can be realised by reducing action to measurements supported by basic theories. On this basis such research proceeds to recommend changes and then is puzzled why the outcome is not always or only the improvement that is predicted! Our inclination is to seek to understand situations as participants see them rather than as theory might suggest and to recognise that once we start to study them we inevitably become part of the situation ourselves, not apart from it.

It follows that we do not see 'qualitative methods' as a set of alternative devices to be found in the researcher's toolbox, but as quite different in character and practice from other methods. 'Research', we suggest, is not a technical set of specialist skills but implicit in social action and close to the ways in which we act in everyday life, for we find increasingly that the worlds of academe and social life, theory and practice, work and family are not really so different but constantly interrupt one another, often in complex ways. Those whose concerns are practice-oriented find that at work there is often a need to deal with 'academic' discourse and to acknowledge academic concerns, for instance, when applying for grants, when negotiating ethics committees, when seeking publication, institutional support, external justification or answering critics. At home, we find ourselves having to respond to policy documents sent to us as parents of children in school, expected to participate in local planning decisions and then sometimes to face questions from journalists.

Discussing issues in reporting research before you have begun and raising the question of how best to deal with the media might seem premature (dealing with the media is a topic rarely addressed in standard texts) but this is less and less the case. Given the wide range of current publications, local and national, print and electronic, we find increasingly that the media make greater demands on research at times of their choosing and that these demands are increasingly theoretical, since they seem more and more often to be about one thing superficially and other things beneath the surface. Like research, no longer do the media just want 'the facts'; they are searching for stories.

The increasing interest of the media in research is only one instance of a need to rethink the relationships between those who do research and those who have it done to them. Until very recently most of us probably thought of our relationship to research being that of only a minor subject – restricted to the fact that we might complete a questionnaire for a large company or a government agency or perhaps find that our use of a credit card had led us to be entered on a commercially available data base. Increasingly, though, we find we need to be not just 'subjects', but competent consumers and users of research. As information technology delivers to us more information than we can easily handle and as the situations in which we live and work become more transient, unpredictable and volatile, the idea that research is concerned only with developing routines for collecting and categorising information has become inadequate. Research (and evaluation) involves asking questions that are no longer just the concern of specialists but have become ubiquitous demands made on many people in many circumstances; demands that are not just technical but which have social, political and moral implications. At the same time, the techniques and methods of research available have changed very little. Just as teachers tend, when under pressure, to teach as they were taught, so most of us, faced with a demand from someone above us in the organisation for research or for an evaluation report, find that our reflex response is to put together a questionnaire and attempt to conduct a survey, usually on limited, or more often non-existent, resources.

In this book we will suggest some ways you can begin to build a continuing research dimension into your work. We have suggested ideas that need not be too demanding but which will be useful in helping you to develop a deeper understanding of some of the situations in which you find yourself. Small-scale surveys carried out under pressure are only rarely of more than transient use or interest and often succeed only in irritating their subjects. Here we have tried to suggest ways of doing research that we have found engage people's interest and enthusiasm and which often have led to new ways of thinking, new possibilities for action and sometimes a new sense of direction.

While research and evaluation have become everyday concerns for many, within the universities, the traditional home of research, academic courses are everywhere attempting to become more vocational in orientation.

'Scholarship', the central value in academic research, finds itself under threat as universities rethink the relations between education and training, and between training and employment, and as conventional boundaries between disciplines diminish in the face of a research world that is increasingly cross- or multi-disciplinary. The last few years have been a time of great change in universities throughout the world. Some people who have moved from government or industry to work in a university are surprised to discover that working in a university means they do less research, and the research that they do is treated less seriously than in their previous workplace. Coming to the university, they acquire the identity of researchers, but lose an effective research role.

In all these changes (which we have sketched only briefly) there are points of convergence between 'academic' and 'practical' research. As an 'academic' researcher you can be called to account to non-specialists for the utility and value of your research often at short notice and in mid-project, while, as a 'practical' researcher, you can face demands that derive as much from academic as from practical concerns. You may be asked to relate an action project to an area of the research literature, expected to meet the requirements of a particular experimental design and asked to frame and express outcomes in ways that do not match with your intentions.

These changes in the way we think about research, in teaching and in training, in the social and health services and in a wide range of community agencies, call for new skills that go beyond some competence in sampling, questionnaire design and being able to manipulate and present figures. Being intellectually agile in moving from one way of thinking and talking about research to another; maintaining commitment and enthusiasm when pressure is being applied by those who perceive what you are doing as threatening; sustaining some concern for the process when the demand is

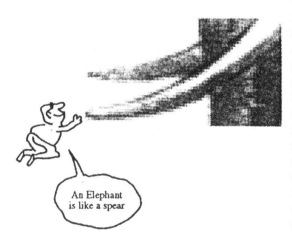

for a mundane product; finding ways to incorporate those who make evaluation demands as participants in the program rather than accepting their view of themselves as consumers of it; thinking of research as providing space for reflection rather than as a means for extending the scope of coercion – these and other survival skills have become necessary accomplishments for many social researchers, inside and outside the university.

WHO ARE WE?

As the demarcations blur between research that is pure and applied, academic and practical, scholastic and immediately useful, so we need to rethink the role of the researcher. In qualitative research particularly, as the role becomes less specialised, less highly tuned to a specific focus and less insulated from other forms of work, so the identity of the researcher becomes diffused. Relinquishing claims to specialised expertise, being less clear about what aspects of the role are social and what are personal, lacking the security of stable paradigms and accepted methods throws the researcher back on personal resources; imaginative, cognitive and moral. As the insulation between the role and identity breaks down, so conventional values of objectivity, claims to truth and community of enquiry have to be rethought and reconstructed.

Conventionally, researchers have not admitted to personal interests in their research, except in disclosures that are near-Hollywood-style (i.e. concerned with identifying villains, victims and heroes) but in recent years this has changed as we have realised that the research and the researcher are inextricably locked together, even in the 'natural' sciences. Allowing researchers personal concerns licenses them to practise in new ways but also requires them to be increasingly accountable. Once we admit that, as researchers, we hold values that affect the research that we do, we have to find ways to scrutinise our actions and our motives more closely. Who the researcher is can no longer be left out of the account without jeopardising the validity of the enquiry. So, who are we? You will learn more about us as you read this book, but here is a start:

Michael: When I was a student I used to work as a ski instructor during my term holidays. I started off teaching the beginners' classes, which confronted me with the art of introducing novices into the art of standing on the skis and doing their first wobbly turns on the slope. I soon realised that it was better not to do this as a theorist, explaining all the details of how to stand upright and bend the knees (which I often heard other instructors do with a rising loudness of their voice accompanying their growing impatience). I found that it was better giving beginners the confidence that they could do it. Of course, it was necessary for them to learn how to avoid leaning forward too much and so getting into an awkward position but they picked that up easier if I showed it to them rather than if I explained it in great detail (leaving them standing even longer in the cold). What they needed most was the belief that they could do it. And I think that is true for any learning situation be it a mundane one like skiing or doing research.

Learning and teaching languages helped me a lot too. When I learnt English as a foreign language in school I knew a lot about the language, its history and culture, but I did not know how to ask for knives and forks and other daily necessities. There I realised 'knowing about' is not enough to gain competence in using what you have learnt. When I became a language teacher myself I started looking for ways to make learners aware of what it means to use what they have learnt in meaningful situations. Using methods like psychodrama in language learning opened up new horizons to me in experiencing that learning is always a total human activity. Having moved into teaching research has made me aware that this is no different.

Rob: One of the things that influenced me early in my academic life was that, as a science student in the early 1960s, I became involved in organising a student group that was based at the Royal Court Theatre in London. This might seem incidental, but seeing the ways actors, writers, designers, musicians and others worked, getting involved in improvisation workshops and above all listening to stories, caused me to reflect on the way I had been taught science. It was as though all I had been taught (especially theory) had the effect of creating distance between me and science, not giving me any sense of real competence as a player, only as someone in the audience. In the way I was taught science there was no feeling of becoming a part of the culture of science. When, much later, I found myself teaching research I wanted to find ways of doing so that involved students in doing real research, of feeling that they were, even in a small way, researchers. This is perhaps similar to you wanting the beginners to feel that were really skiing, that they were skiers. But your aside about the raised voices of the other instructors prompts me to ask about institutional support, for there is only so much you can do as an individual teacher.

Michael: Our department has had a long tradition in practising more open forms of research or what has recently been called qualitative research. I guess it goes back to a time when there was still a political movement to try and make the research process more democratic, not only in the relationship between the researcher and the research 'subject' but also among the researchers them-

selves. We were tired of following a sterile pattern of delivering research results in which the voices of the people involved no longer appeared. This struggle has, of course, also had an influence on the politics of whole university departments in Austria, where mainstream research still follows a conventional empirical stance. And students who have been involved in what was going on in the research arena were no longer able to see research as a mere process of applying what they have learnt in an instrumental way.

Rob: I have been fortunate to work in three departments which, in different ways and at different times, have had radical educational traditions. First, at the Centre for Science Education in London, which developed a training course for science teachers which was more consistently experientially based than any other course of its kind I have seen. Second, at the University of East Anglia where, with Barry MacDonald and others, we developed a set of procedures for using qualitative research methods in the context of democratic principles. And, more recently, at Deakin University where we have developed a range of distance programs for teachers and others which are built on action research and action learning models. Each of these moves has not just been from one university to another but has been associated with major changes in my life.

Michael: Stepping out of my own surroundings has been a regular feature in my professional life. Spending some of my time with people of other disciplines such as sociology, nursing and biology and visiting scientific communities in other countries like Britain, the USA and Australia has not only helped me to cross the narrow borders of my own research experience but also widened my horizon in a more general sense. However, I also noticed how difficult it can be to include everything, especially when I think of recent workshops which I held in Estonia or in the war zone between Croatia and Serbia in former Yugoslavia. In places like that I eventually learnt that it is not possible to keep theory apart from practice. What's the point of doing research there if it does not have any effect on the immediate situation?

Rob: The significance of doing research as a response to social change is important and we should ensure that this is a constant theme in the book. Other questions that come to my mind which I would like to include are:

- Questions about the nature and limits of description, for instance, what does it mean to be 'documentary'?
- Questions about the nature of authorship, for instance, what is the nature of the authority vested in the writer of a descriptive account?
- Questions about the role of the reader. Writing and reading are complementary but very different; what happens when we disrupt the demarcation between the researcher as writer and the audience as reader?

These questions are important to me in the areas where I work most at present, that is in environmental education and in evaluating drug education programs, but I would like to know if you feel they are important in working in places like Estonia or Croatia?

Michael: In these places you feel that change is happening but you cannot identify the agent of change. In parts of former Yugoslavia this has become what might be called societal trauma. This makes it very difficult to act as an outsider coming in, for people there have had enough of those researchers who arrive there and try to impose concepts on the situation which are derived from somewhere else. In order to pay attention to the context, I treated action, research and learning as interwoven parts of a process in which participation was a prerequisite. This helped in getting everybody involved, but I am not sure if this can be conveyed in book form.

ACTING EDUCATIVELY

For both of us, most of our professional work has been with teachers, with schools and with other educational organisations, but while our academic location is in education, we aspire to work in ways that are more generally

educational than this normally suggests. Once, it was more or less true
that most of those studying in the
education faculties of universities
were, or intended to become, teachers in schools, even if they later
moved to other jobs. Not only have
schools themselves changed but,
increasingly, we find that our students come from a wider range of
occupations: they are people who
work in hospitals and in other
health care settings, in universities,
the military, in a wide range of non-
government agencies, in the media,
commerce and business organisa-

tions, in the arts and in industry. Their concerns are not always to teach
or to train in the conventional sense but to understand better their
educative role as a part of what it means to be a university teacher,
nurse, community drama producer, social worker, health promotions cam-
paigner, peace activist, journalist, environmentalist, military, police or
prison officer, general practitioner or personnel manager. Most of our
students also find that one experience they have in common is that they
find themselves drawn increasingly into the ambit of government and
institutional research as they are required to develop proposals, evaluate
programs and document their work: tasks for which they often turn to
educational case studies for an appropriate and congenial answer.

The educational world may once have been solely concerned with
questions about schools and schooling, but it has changed. The collapse
of the conventional distinctions between the worlds of publishing, computing and the media foretold by Nicholas Negroponte (and described in
Stewart Brand's book, *The Media Lab*) are beginning to have far-reaching
consequences for education. Contemporary cultures are increasingly educative in nature, defined and driven by their capability to create, select,
transmit, transform and evaluate knowledge, and by their capacity to
sustain a highly specialised, fragmented, fast-changing and eclectic knowledge base. Our contemporary societies are thus caught between the need
for common knowledge and the drive towards particular fragments of
specialist and esoteric knowledge; education tries to bridge some of the
gaps. Teachers have been at the forefront in these changes – think, for
instance, of the enormous input (much of it voluntary labour) in training in
information technology in the last ten years, of the investment that has
been needed in language training as a consequence of large-scale migration
and the appearance of new large-scale economic infrastructures like those

in the EU, of the shift (in many countries) to new forms of political life and the rethinking that has been faced in many 'families' about how best to manage childcare in new social and economic circumstances.

Increasingly, more and more of us depend for our survival on working with cultural knowledge in fast-changing circumstances. Even a decade ago, when information was comparatively scarce, our culture a relatively fixed feature of our lives and social conditions (for some at least) seemed more stable, research was largely concerned with the collection, sifting and categorisation of information. Now, in fast-changing times, information is ubiquitous and cheap. Neil Postman (in 1990) wrote:

> In America, there are 260,000 billboards; 11,520 newspapers; 11,556 periodicals; 27,000 video outlets for renting tapes; 362 million tv-sets; and over 400 million radios. There are 40,000 new book titles published every year (300,000 world-wide) and every day in America 41 million photographs are taken, and just for the record, over 60 billion pieces of advertising junk mail come into our mail boxes every year. Everything from telegraphy and photography in the 19th century to the silicon chip in the twentieth has amplified the din of information, until matters have reached such proportions today that for the average person, information no longer has any relation to the solution of problems. The tie between information and action has been severed. Information is now a commodity that can be bought and sold, or used as a form of entertainment, or worn like a garment to enhance one's status. It comes indiscriminately, directed at no one in particular, disconnected from usefulness; we are glutted with information, drowning in information, have no control over it, don't know what to do with it.
>
> (Postman, address to a conference in 1990; a similar and publicly accessible quote can be found in Postman 1993: 68)

But we do not have to become the passive (and humourless) consumers of the mass media Neil Postman assumes; 'research', in the way we have

defined it, gives us a way to recover and to reconstruct meaning in our lives. As information becomes mass produced for all, research has necessarily to be redefined as a wide-ranging process concerned not just with finding what is new, but with finding what may be significant in what is already known, with looking critically at the ways

in which knowledge is traded and exchanged, valued, recycled and reprocessed. Simply to collect information is now a trivial task. For research, the
key task is now more often to find ways of rejecting information that is of
little use than it is of collecting yet more; to be critical may be a more
important role for research than to be rigorous.

Central to the new role of research that has emerged are the changes that
have taken place in the professions. Where research was once seen as the
handmaiden to professional practice, the move to greater public account-
ability, organisationally pervasive forms of financial stringency and the
diffusion of educational and training concerns through a broad range of
social institutions has required kinds of research that are somewhat less
pure and innocent than academic researchers might seek for themselves.
Without our active intervention, research becomes, one way or another, an
instrument of the state. No longer solely defined by the values of scholarship and contained within the academy, the politicisation of research has
been accelerated by demographic, workplace and employment changes. It is
marked too by a growing separation of the management of professional
work from the work itself, so creating the need for better information
about the delivery of services and the emergence of a discourse about the
'delivery' and 'quality' of service which is very different from the ways that
practitioners and clients talk about what they do and what they value. Not
surprisingly, in almost all current discussions of professional education and
training, political issues are close to the surface and gender issues always
close at hand.

BEING REFLEXIVE ABOUT BEING REFLEXIVE

This book is about research, but about a particular form of research,
concerned to counter the tendency for research to become the currency
of institutional power. First, it is about research in relation to practice. This
is not to say it intends only to be practical, but it is concerned with research
that makes a difference to the ways in which people work, think about their
work and relate to others. Second, it is concerned with questions of
methodology rather than with questions only of method. Our aim is not
to write another research methods recipe book but to treat the methods of
research as much a part of the subject of research as substantive issues.

While we want the book to be practical, we mean by this that it should
involve the critical application of the methods we describe and close
attention to the evaluation of their consequences and effects. In any
practical situation that calls for research there is a strong temptation to
do research that is method-led. This is true for those who come to research
as beginners and who look for problems which appear to fit the methods
with which they feel most comfortable but it is also true for experienced

researchers, who will often look for an angle or a perspective that similarly allows them to construe a problem in such a way that it fits a pattern that is familiar and manageable. The significance of the use of the term 'methodology' is that it requires an argument to connect the choice and practice of particular methods to the way that the problem is conceived and the utility and limitations of the outcome. It is in this sense of the term, as requiring a critical justification for the adoption and practice of particular research methods, that we claim that our concern is with 'methodology' rather than with methods alone.

This does, of course, create a problem for us as writers, for in a book about research methods, it is possible, indeed it has become conventional, to describe a range of different methods as context-free, to treat them as abstractions and to connect them to practice only by using illustrative examples. Only rarely do books on research methods discuss situations in which particular methods should not be used, or situations within which the methods chosen may cause distortion or precipitate changes that are not captured by the methods themselves. Think of the example of opinion polls as used in political campaigns. Such polls have come to create a reality of their own, they have become an intrinsic, even indispensable part of the political process, but the methodological concerns of those who do this research appear to be mainly with questions internal to the method. They worry about sampling designs, about the reliability of their instruments and the consistency of the interviewer's behaviour. They appear to worry less, in public at least, about methodological issues of the kind that would prompt them to ask how the use of these methods and the selective publication of their results might affect the political process. Such questions are seen to lie elsewhere – with those who commission and use the research rather than with those who conduct it.

Throughout this book we will resist, when we can, the temptation to focus only on technical issues arising from the use of research methods. We believe this market-driven and technical view of research is misplaced; it leads to a view of research as a product and to those who pay for it as only consumers, which has as one consequence a view of the researcher as an expert in instruments, a view we know to be inherently flawed. Methodology is too important to be left to the researcher: just as we look for shared responsibility for research, so we believe researchers have the responsibility to participate in discussions about the commissioning, use and application of research, despite the criticism that to do so threatens to undermine their objectivity – a theme to which we will return.

A central problem we face in writing about research methods in a way that draws attention to methodological issues is that of finding a form that is reflexive. Reflexive in the sense that it provides us with ways of talking about research on practice that treats research itself as practice. We need to find ways of turning our approach to research back on itself so that it becomes critically recursive, and we need to do this in ways that avoid falling into a downward spiral of infinite regression.

Perhaps one clue to a resolution of this problem lies in the form of the previous paragraph. On reflection, it is written in a way that invites the reader to collude in a persuasive fiction woven by the writer. At this moment, as we write, the cursor moves across a blank screen and the text that is to follow remains not just hidden but unknown. But this is not the case for the reader, who is located at another point in time and for whom the text that follows is already fixed. (You can look to the end to see what happens, but we can't!) The usual device adopted by those who write textbooks about research methods is to strive to create the fiction that the writer and the reader occupy locations in narrative space that are disconnected from social life. There is a sense of timelessness, or at least the suggestion that writer and reader are time-free, that characterises much academic writing. The 'text', both reader and writer assume, exists in a world of its own, contained by its

covers. Books on research methods, therefore, tend to be like manuals, consisting mainly of procedures and instructions to be followed. Though often when these instructions are followed the consequences are not quite those given in the illustrations, just as the illustrations in cookery books rarely include the clearing up that remains to be done, or mention the multiple agendas that actually typify the operations of the domestic economy, allowing for feeding cat, answering the 'phone or entertaining young children in mid-soufflé.

The solution we propose to the problem of creating a reflexive text about research is that just as we assume the reader to be concerned with research problems whose particular form we do not know and in a time and place that is distant from this keyboard on a desk in Austr[al]ia, so we should locate this text in ways that are more specific than accounts of research method alone can provide. We want to avoid where we can the problem of retrospective reconstruction. There are books in which researchers describe the process of their research autobiographically, and often they provide the most valuable accounts for those concerned with research practice. Examples include Okely and Callaway (1992), who provide a collection of recent papers on the theme; Hortense Powdermaker (1967), who was both a trade unionist and anthropologist; Helen Simons (1987), who provides some interesting correspondence she has had as an evaluator with officials in school systems. George Spindler (1988) has collected accounts from ethnographers working in education and Martyn Hammersley (1983) has 'exposed' the truth about his PhD thesis. There are also one or two books which take the further step of recreating research as fiction; Alison Lurie (1967), Elenore Smith Bowen (a pseudonym adopted by anthropologist Laura Bohannen) (1954), Malcolm Bradbury (1993b) and David Lodge (1989) for instance. But the fact that such books are set aside from the mainstream of research can mean that what they have to say to researchers themselves may be ignored. If we are to make research democratic then we have to find ways to break the mould that confines research to a highly selected group of specialists; indeed if research itself is to survive the changes we have sketched here this is an urgent task.

What all this will mean for what follows is that instead of presenting the book as disembodied and generalised accounts of research methods, we will write about methods in context. We will describe research in action rather than in abstraction. We will try to repopulate research and research methods. The illustrative examples we will present, instead of following the recipes, will lead them. The narrative style we will employ will be conversational rather than didactic. So, the narrative fiction in which we invite you to collude is not that of an abstracted and disembodied lecture, but imagines that you are sitting alongside us as we write. As the cursor moves across the screen we imagine your reader's eyes following close behind asking questions, making suggestions, taking paths that run off at tangents. So . . . > . . .

2 Elephants and apples: from social perception to false consciousness

This chapter takes as its theme the social nature of perception. In particular it is about the way we respond to situations that generate different readings and multiple interpretations. We say 'respond' rather than simply 'perceive' for, in social situations, 'perception' is not quite the mechanical and passive process it appears to be from reading some psychology texts. We need a new word, a word similar to the idea of 'perception–communication', which David Bohm (1965) has used to bring to social science ideas of indeterminacy derived from particle physics. 'Scientific investigation', he writes, 'is basically a mode of extending our perception of the world and not mainly a mode for obtaining knowledge about it' (Bohm 1965: 129). The point to note is that perception is itself social action and where both perception and communication begin and end is not easily identified.

Most of our experiences of observing social situations, in families, at work, in community settings, on holiday, or in our dealings with such organisations as schools, prisons or hospitals make this plain, but social science is often written from a different perspective. Here situations are not understood from within, from the perspective of a particular role, but from the ideal viewpoint and with the steady gaze of the notionally external observer. From this standpoint, social science may claim to have the keys to truth, or at least to an objectivity that makes truth realisable, but such claims neglect the fact that research is itself socially located, and its claims to truth are more likely than not to become part of the problem rather than a means of finding answers to it. It is therefore necessary for research never to claim the last word and always to be reflexive, to be about itself as well as about its focus of concern.

We will begin this chapter by looking at social perception and the way that it is both embedded in social situations and is itself a social process. This theme, though, presents its own challenges, since 'reading' itself involves social perception. To be consistent we need to find a form for this chapter (indeed for the book) which not only allows the text to be informative but also reflexive. In other words the text needs to take a standpoint that is different from that of the external and objective observer. We need to find a form that places the authors inside events, and allows the reader a sense of access to the writers. We need too a form that disrupts the expectation that theory and practice are discrete and separable and that the gap between cognition and affect can be kept water-tight and heavily insulated. So, rather than presenting a theory and then giving illustrative examples, we will provide accounts of perception in action and then use these to develop a platform from which to develop further ideas.

SPOOR TRACKING

Our first case consists of a trek through the ether following the trail of a legendary elephant. The story we tell will demonstrate that we each perceive objects and events differently, and having perceived them so we are likely to disagree about which direction we should go in search of what might seem the same quarry.

We are grateful to all those members of the listserver 'Qualitative Research Methods for the Human Sciences' <QUALRS-L@uga.bitnet> who contributed to this quest not always knowing our full intention. In what follows we have quoted selectively and edited contributions that were posted in the course of discussion. The exact status of such discussions has been a point of dispute on a number of lists. While Li and Crane (1993) offer a set of procedures for citing contributions, some people have argued that e-mail discussions should be treated as oral rather than literary and it is inappropriate to quote from them in publications. We have contacted all but one person who contributed to ask their permission to quote from them here and all those we have been able to contact have generously agreed. The one person we were unable to contact we have identified by initials and have not named. E-mail communities tend to be transient, if intense, and since many contributors to this list were graduate students at the time of the discussion, they have since moved and cannot easily be traced. Our judgement is that this particular discussion was public rather than private and, given recognition of the context in which comments were made, it is not inappropriate to quote from it here.

The story begins in late January 1992, with Michael explaining his approach to the teaching of research methods and asking a question:

From Michael Schratz, Deakin University, Australia, 21 Jan. 1992
. . . Has anybody out there come across the Indian story of the elephant? . . . The idea is that people get to know an elephant at different parts of the animal and thus encounter it as different 'objects', e.g. for the one who touches the elephant's tail an elephant is like a rope, for the one touching its legs it is like a tree trunk etc. I have a picture of this scene which I usually use in my research classes in Austria but I have never come across the actual text. I'd appreciate it if somebody could tell us where we could find it. . . .

In the next two days thirteen replies were received, many of them offering sightings of the elephant:

From King Beach, Michigan State University, USA, 22 Jan. 1992
I believe (but I am not absolutely certain as there are 547 of them) that the story of the elephant and the blind men derives from the Jataka Tales which are Pali Buddhist scriptures written during the time of Gautama Buddha in India. The tale does present a nice argument for a systems approach in social sciences, though I have never seen it used as such.

From Trish Wilson, McMaster University, Canada, 22 Jan. 1992
I haven't seen the story you are looking for in print for years, what I have experienced is Pete Seeger, the American folksinger, telling the story . . . if you are interested I'll go through my record collection (! yes . . . records!) and give you the complete reference, or if you'd like, I can tape it and send it along . . . .

From Michael Carrithers, University of Durham, UK, 22 Jan. 1992
The story of the wise men and the elephant is one I use frequently in thought and conversation. It appeared in a children's encyclopedia which I think was called the World Book Encyclopedia. I used to pore over it for hours. I recognise that this will hardly impress you as a canonical source. . . .

From Peter Junger, CWRU Law School, 22 Jan. 1992
The story of the blind men and the elephant appears in the Udana, which is part of the Pali Buddhist Canon. It seems that a bunch of philosophers and scholars were discussing the sort of issues that philosophers and scholars have always discussed, and some of the followers of the historical Buddha asked him which opinions were correct. Gautama Buddha responded by telling the story.

From Bob Georges, UCLA, USA, 22 Jan. 1992
The story you asked about is known among folklorists as Type 1317. The Blind Men and Elephant. See Sith Thompson, 'The Types of the Folktale', second revised edition (Helsinki, 1961) . . . .

From Trish Wilson, McMaster University, Canada, 23 Jan. 1992
I will be glad to dig out the record – I need an excuse to indulge in some folk music – however it will be a day or two . . . as I have a thesis due on Friday . . . .

All this was helpful, but conversations on these lists often develop a life of their own. We soon found ourselves thinking of new questions and travelling in unexpected directions:

From Robert Hollon, Wisconsin, USA, 22 Jan. 1992
. . . what might it be like from the perspective of the elephant?

From Art Schwartz, University of Calgary, Canada, 22 Jan. 1992
The elephant is truly a wondrous beast. But the thing that should be generating wonder about the old story of the visually-handicapped observers and the elephant is NOT that each of the blind folk perceived the elephant differently. Rather the lesson in the tale lies in what it demonstrates about the arrogance and folly of the narrator who assumes that only he/she is capable of accurately perceiving the true nature of the animal.

From Art Schwartz, University of Calgary, 23 Jan. 1992
. . . an elephantine mystery . . . .

Inspired by the response Michael set off for the library. He found several versions of the story, both translations of the original and versions translated for English-speaking children. Here are two examples:

The first version is from the *Undana* (Woodward 1985: 82–3)

. . . there was a certain rajah . . . that rajah called to a certain man, saying, 'Come thou, good fellow, go and gather together in one place all the men in Savatthi who were born blind.'

'Very good sire,' replied that man, and in obedience to the rajah gathered together all the men born blind in Savatthi, and having done so, went to the rajah and said, 'Sire, all the men born blind in Savatthi are assembled.'

'Then, my good man, show the blind men an elephant.'

'Very good sire,' said the man, and did as he was told, and said to them, 'O blind, such as this is an elephant'; and to one man he presented the head of the elephant, to another its ear, to another a tusk, to another the trunk, the foot, back, tail and tuft of the tail, saying to each one that this was the elephant.

Now, monks, that man, having thus presented the elephant to the blind men, came to the rajah and said, 'Sire, the elephant has been presented to the blind men. Do what is your will.'

Thereupon, monks, that rajah went up to the blind men and said to each, 'Well blind man, have you seen the elephant?'

'Yes, sire.'

'Then tell me, blind men, what sort of thing is an elephant.'

Thereupon those who had been presented with the head answered, 'Sire, an elephant is like a pot.' And those who had observed an ear only replied, 'An elephant is like a winnowing-basket.' Those who had been presented with a tusk said it was a ploughshare. Those who knew only the trunk said it was a plough; they said that the body was a granary; the foot, a pillar; the back, a mortar; the tail, a pestle; the tuft of the tail just a besom.

Then they began to quarrel, shouting, 'Yes, it is!' 'No, it is not!' 'An elephant is not that!' 'Yes, it's like that!' and so on until they came to fisticuffs over the matter. Then, monks, this rajah was delighted with the scene.

'Just so are these Wanderers holding other views, blind, unseeing, knowing not the profitable, knowing not the unprofitable . . . . In their ignorance of these things they are by nature quarrelsome, wrangling and disputatious, each maintaining it is thus and thus.'

Thereupon, the Exalted One . . . seeing the meaning of it, gave utterance to this verse of uplift:

> O how they cling and wrangle, some who claim
> Of brahmin and recluse the honoured name!
> For quarrelling, each to his view cling.
> Such folk see only one side of thing.

This next version is from the first edition of the *Victorian Readers* (Saxe 1930), published in Melbourne for use in schools:

> *The Blind Men and the Elephant*
> A Hindu fable
>
> It was six men of Hindustan, To learning much inclined,
> Who went to see the elephant
> (Though all of them were blind),
> That each by observation
> Might satisfy the mind.
>
> The first approached the elephant,
> And happening to fall
> Against its broad and sturdy side,
> At once began to bawl:
> 'Why, bless me! but the elephant
> Is very like a wall!'
>
> The second, as he felt the tusk,
> Cried, 'Ho! what have we here
> So very round and smooth and sharp?

To me 'tis mighty clear
This wonder of an elephant
Is very like a spear.'

The third approached the animal,
And happening to take
The squirming trunk within his hand,
Thus boldly up he spake:
'I see,' quoth he, 'the elephant
Is very like a snake!'

The fourth reached out his eager hand,
And felt about its knee.
'What most this wondrous beast is like
Is mighty plain,' quoth he:
''Tis clear enough the elephant
Is very like a tree!'

The fifth, who chanced to touch the ear,
Said, 'E'en the blindest man
Can tell what this resembles most;
Deny the fact who can
This marvel of an elephant
Is very like a fan!'

The sixth no sooner had begun
About the beast to grope,
Than, seizing on the swinging tail
That fell within his scope,
'I see,' quoth he, 'the elephant
Is very like a rope!'

And so these men of Hindustan
Disputed loud and long,
Each in his own opinion
Exceeding stiff and strong;
Though each of them was partly in the right,
They all of them were wrong!

This looked like a point of closure on the story, but we underestimated the power of the elephant story to recur, and in particular the story's happy knack of always being about itself. It seems it is impossible to stand apart from the story and comment upon it, because as soon as you do, the elephant reconstitutes itself before your eyes!

A few days after our first enquiry, the elephant was seen again, this time

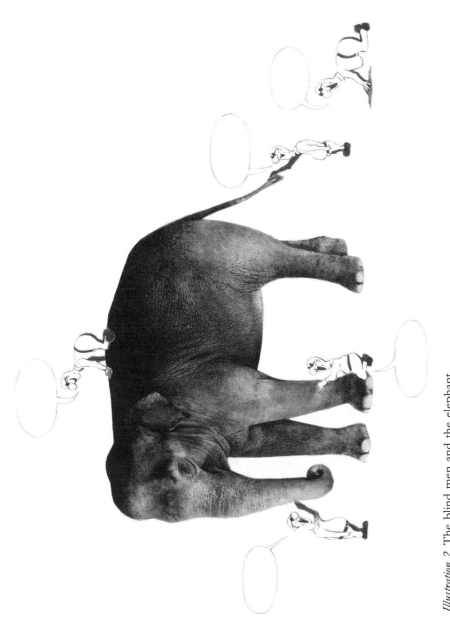

Illustration 2 The blind men and the elephant

in Oregon (which some will know is close to Big Foot country) and created something of a stampede in the networks . . .

From Yu-mei Wang, Oregon, USA, 6 Feb. 1992
One day, one of my classmates showed a picture of six blind men with an elephant. He said that quantitative research is like the six blind men. They (quantitative researchers) study only one part of the elephant, but they generalise their result to the whole elephant. Qualitative researchers just study one small part (for example, one leg), they do not try to generalise. But I do not think it is true. Because quantitative researchers must be very careful in identifying the relevant population. If they decide to study one leg, they can only generalise to the other legs, not to other parts of the elephant . . . .

But the posting that really provoked responses was this one, less concerned with the elephant than with the political correctness of involving blind men in the story:

Mary Kay Schleiter, UWP, USA, 6 Feb. 1992
I object to the term 'six blind men' to mean narrow-mindedness. A person with a visual impairment is no more narrow-minded than anyone else. The use of this false analogy perpetuates negative stereotypes. I know it wasn't meant that way. If I ever make a similarly insensitive remark, I would appreciate being called on it.

Stan Yoder, 6 Feb. 1992
. . . I entirely agree that someone with a visual impairment is no more narrowminded than anyone else; the point is, however, that by definition they see less clearly than those without impairment. . . .

Mary Kay Schleiter, UWP, USA, 6 Feb. 1992
Stan, you haven't convinced me. A person with visual impairment usually has sharper perception than usual in their other senses and 'sees' differently than those without visual impairment, but not necessarily 'less clearly'. I do not like the analogy, and I believe it is insensitive, inaccurate, and harmful.

George Balch, UICVM, 6 Feb. 1992
. . . it has nothing whatsoever to do with blind people in a literal way at all. Nor does it deal with 'handicapped' people in any literal way. It is purely analogical . . . .

Ran Pleasant, Catholic University of America, 7 Feb. 1992
. . . In my opinion the term 'blind men' can refer to nothing but blind

men – 'literally' . . . references to 'blind men' or any other handicapped, minority, or majority groups has no place in professional research.

Bruce Jones, UCSD, 7 Feb. 1992
Blind; adj.   1. – without the power of sight; unable to see; sightless,

   2. – or of sightless persons,

   3. – not able or willing to notice, understand or judge,

   4. – done without adequate directions or knowledge [a blind search]

   5. – disregarding evidence, sound logic eye [blind love, blind faith]

   Webster's New World Dictionary, Third College Edition, New York: Simon & Schuster, 1988

   Well, which 'literal' blindness do you like? Perhaps in the case of the parable of the blind men and the elephant, they were just unable to see what was 'literally' in front of their noses.

Mikko Mantysaari, University of Tampere, Finland, 7 Feb. 1992
Do you MEAN that it is forbidden to refer to visually impaired people as 'blind' when we are doing research? Or should we pretend that there is no such thing as 'blindness' . . . ?

George Balch, UICVM, 8 Feb. 1992
[addressed to Mary Kay and Ran] I'm not sure what you are objecting to, and trust you know none of us in this discussion intend to offend anyone. So let me try again. If we substitute 'people who are unable to see the elephant' for blind men – perhaps because it is dark or they arc wearing opaque lenses . . . would that still be offensive?

John Seidel, 7 Feb. 1992
. . . the issue is the cultural resources that we draw upon to formulate the epistemological problem, and the unreflective way we draw upon them . . . the story works because it draws on stereotypes and stigmas that have plagued people-who-happen-to-be-blind for a long time. Their personhood has always been subjugated to their blindness.

Peter Junger, CWRU Law School, 8 Feb. 1992
For heaven's sake. The story of the blind men and the elephant is not just part of our culture . . . [it] is two thousand five hundred years old and part of the Buddhist canon. . . . You are going to have to burn a lot of books and kill a lot of Thais to get it to go away.

   . . . I cannot imagine that any blind person has ever been upset by this story – are any of those who complain of its use actually blind?

John Seidel, 10 Feb. 1992
. . . for me the problem is not what words or parables meant 2,500 years ago, or in another language, or in another culture . . . what matters is what words, signs, symbols or stories mean here and now, and the consequences of continuing to use them.

. . . After doing research among people who happen to be deaf . . . I was shocked and surprised to learn that [for them] the phrase 'deaf and dumb' is the equivalent of a racial slur. I was guilty of it. I don't think that people who are deaf particularly care about the linguistic roots of the phrase. . . .

If you start looking at the literature in this area, you will begin to see the pejorative character of the phrase . . . and the extent to which some social science work is grounded in, and perpetuates, the pejorative sense of this phrase.

I think this is part of the larger problem of doing qualitative/ethnographic research and analysis. The intelligibility, plausibility and acceptability of our work . . . involves our use of unexplicated, taken-for-granted resources in our writing . . . .

In order to get on with the work, we frequently make use of these things in unreflected upon ways . . . but ignoring them . . . can result in . . . potentially damaging work.

When researchers get into academic debates of a philosophical kind, someone will almost always suggest that a simple resolution to the debate may lie in an empirical test.

G. W., California, 11 Feb. 1992
. . . I sent the debate on the 6 blind men and the elephant to two people who are blind . . . I think their replies will be of interest . . . .

But sometimes it is more difficult to ask the question than it might first seem:

Tzipporah Ben-Avraham, Brooklyn, 11 Feb. 1992
OK Gary. I am NOT a BLIND 'MAN'. I am a blind WOMAN! . . . GIVE ME A BREAK!

Even when the right question is asked of the right person, the answer may still offer some sense of surprise:

Norm Coombs, Rochester Institute, 11 Feb. 1992
Yes, I am blind and have been for 51 years. . . . Actually a few years ago there was an elephant on display at a shopping centre. We stopped to show our kids. My wife wasn't going close and stayed in the car. . . .

Daddy was brave and went. I got to feel his trunk and was amazed at the stiff bristles like a hard hairbrush. Well maybe I tickled its trunk but I barely turned around when he SNEEZED! Yes he sneezed in upper case and I almost had a heart attack.

If you are not familiar with electronic networks, then this discussion may give you some idea of the advantages and the drawbacks of becoming a user. This list is one of many, often highly specialised, virtual talking shops. You will see that people can be incredibly helpful, that information that might take hours of library research can often be gained very quickly by posting a request. But you will see too that there is no controlling the discussion once it reaches critical mass. On most lists there are periodic bursts of activity like the one we have included here. The course of their progress is quite unpredictable, and like an elephant, unstoppable, the only thing to do is to follow wherever it leads. But at this point we will leave the trail to pick up the elephant in another guise.

A DESCRIPTION OF THE EXPERIMENT

The account that follows is of a teaching experiment we have used on a number of different occasions to demonstrate the complex social interactions and trails of ideas that lead from the observation, implicit in the story of the blind men and the elephant, that perceptions are always partial.

From a group, three people are selected or asked to volunteer. They are asked to sit, side-by-side in a row facing the audience. Then they are blindfolded and told that they will each be asked to touch an object, an everyday object that they would recognise instantly if they saw it. The group leader then takes out a segment of an apple (a half or quarter) which has been cut with a knife some time before – it is important that the cut surface has dried and that the smell of the fruit is not too easily identifiable. It is important too that the segment retains the stalk.

The group leader then approaches the first blindfolded person, takes hold of their index finger and guides it to touch (briefly and softly) part of the apple (as in Illustration 3a). The leader then repeats this with each of the three, each time guiding them to touch a different part of the apple – the smooth skin, the cut surface, the stalk, perhaps an edge. On the basis of one brief touch of the object the group are then asked to discuss what they felt and what they think it was that they touched. They can remove their blindfolds to do this, but the apple should be well-hidden!

We have tried this exercise with different groups, adults and children, and, while the event plays out differently every time, the account that follows is typical.

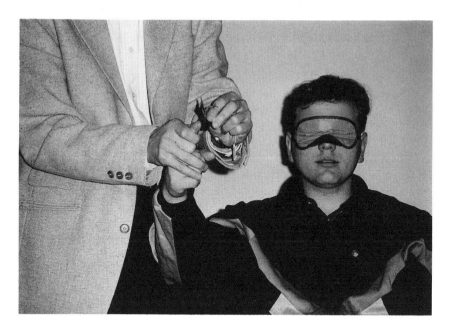

(a)

(b)

Illustration 3 Two photographs of the 'experiment'

What is it?

It feels like a – [reaches down and touches foot]
It's rough
Dry
It's soft
It's not smooth
It's like a cat's tongue! But not so rough!
It's soft
It wasn't soft
It was dry
It wasn't wet
It wasn't hard
It's like velvet
No
It was dry
It's like the bottom of a banana [miming banana shape in the air]
It's composed of something hard
It's composed of something soft
[pause]
I can't think of anything
Maybe it is part of a bag [pointing to a bag lying on the table behind]
It was drier
It had no texture
Could it be flesh? [reaching down to touch his bare foot]
Foot? [runs finger along edge of big toenail]
No, not this [touches skin at the base of his heel]
It doesn't fit into your conception
It was so dry
It was like a plaster
Something similar
Kiwi! It was like a kiwi skin.
Good, it was soft
Not according to me!
[pause]
It is difficult!
[pause]
Can we feel it again?
[They each feel a second time, not necessarily at the same spot]
It feels like a part of human flesh – a finger?
No, not a finger!
Wait, like skin . . .
Cooler
Really dry. Was it an apple?

Apple? [in disbelief]
Fruit, something fresh
No
No
Could be an orange
Scratchy, an apple is too smooth
Can we ask questions?
[Michael] Of course, you are the research team.
Skin-like?
I know a lot about food! It's not a french fry!
Bread sticks
Could it be food?
It's compact – not like skin
Can I feel your finger? The object was harder than this
[Michael gives out pens] Sometimes when they are doing research researchers try to write about or draw what they have found.
[The three begin to write words – tough, smooth, skin – someone touches the surface of the paper]
Not paper, it's too dry
An apple? An orange?
[Drawings of lines and comments like soft, flat, straight, hard]
How do you fit the impressions together?
Could one object have different parts?

Next day we showed this transcript to a group that included some who were not there and who had only the transcript, some had observed the incident and three were the people who participated in the exercise. When we asked those who had not been involved in the incident, either as blindfolded participants or as observers, what was happening they quickly identified it as an illustration of a familiar problem – that of being faced with the task of trying to reach agreement on selective and partial evidence. They saw the three participants as talking but not listening to one another:

It seems there were only two people. One was thinking about food while the other was thinking about the human body. They had a dialogue/ argument on what they felt, however the words they used to describe the object were similar.

They are not able to listen to each other. They are not able to include another person's impression and build a comprehensive model of the object. They are also not able to take the other person's position (a lack of empathy). Interaction between them is not effective, actually there is no interaction.

This is a frustrating experience that is typical of people interacting. They are sensing in some form the same object but cannot describe it to

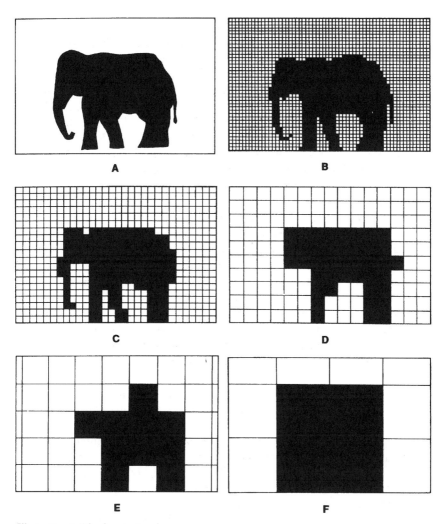

Illustration 4 Elephant pixcels
Note: The number of picture points determines the resolution: A = very large – print screen
(B = 2400, C= 600, D = 150, E = 37.5, F = 9.4 picture points – after K. Steinbuch)
Source: Legewie and Ehlers *Knaurs moderne Psychologie* © 1972 (new edition 1992), Munich:
Droemer Knaur Verlag

another because they only have their subjective experience to draw upon. It shows how limited people are in truly communicating their own experience and sensation to others. We try to connect a new experience to some past one or to some frame of reference but this is very limiting.

The interaction might be seen as like a political meeting, or a parody of such a formal meeting. All that matters is what you say, the object itself is unimportant. It's a kind of social petting.

Those who had observed the discussion were able to fill in much of the detail not available to those who saw only the transcript, but their account of the process was basically similar. Here is a typical example:

> Three researchers/students are attempting to come to a conclusion as to what the object is that they have touched. The three touched different parts of an apple. They were blindfolded. After taking off their blindfolds, a discussion takes place. 'It feels like this', 'It feels like that' . . . . They argue over their perceptions, assuming that they cannot all be right. The two males either always begin the discussion or are very emphatic about their conclusion. The female takes time to think and does not lead the discussion. Many adjectives and similes are used to describe the object. Pens are provided. They write the adjectives on the board. Then it is suggested that maybe they should draw instead. The words on the board seem to limit and bring to a standstill their discussion. I sense a slight frustration. In the end the object is revealed – it is an apple. The food expert, Douglas, had initially come to this conclusion. The others were not convinced. They had all touched different parts of the apple (inside, outside, stem) and were not able to conclude that possibly one object has different surfaces (like most objects do). Arguments directed the discussion. Each researcher's perception was the final conclusion – they were unable to believe the others' perceptions.

When we come to the accounts given by the participants an important shift occurs. Here are three accounts from this particular experiment:

1 The experience of being a subject of research was a very interesting one. Trying to make a comparison of your own experience with others' experiences gives you the possibility of finding out how difficult it is to harmonise perceptions about one thing.
2 My experience was just getting the perception of an object, just touching a tiny part of it. In this case it was a part (the stem) that because of its texture was totally different from the other parts of the object. My head started working when I noticed that according to our experiences we were talking about different things. So, mentally I started to sum the elements given to create a mental picture of what we were talking about. So I defined the object as a fruit (an apple I thought), but even so I wasn't really sure. Because of this uncertainty I couldn't convince the others about the idea I had about the subject.
3 I was a member of the research group:
   - I found it difficult because of the very, very restricted experience that was allowed, one spot, one touch, one second.
   - It very soon became clear that we had different experiences and were building different theories as to what it was.

- Trying to put a sensual experience into words or into a drawing is very difficult.
- It turned into a two to one discussion because the two of us had a more similar experience than the third.
- The apple didn't fit into my experience because I didn't think of the possibility that an apple could be cut into halves.
- With some time the singular, peculiar experience began to vanish and led to a new experience.
- Verification changed the theory building.
- The value of triangulation that combines seemingly incompatible experiences.

(Students' writing EPU 1993)

In discussion, the blindfolded participants expressed some surprise at the interpretation that they had failed to listen to one another. They said they had concentrated very hard on what others said but that they found it difficult to use what they heard or build on it in any way because they could not find connections to their own experience. They thought too that the other two were listening to them but the lack of any progress in reaching consensus kept pushing them back to their limited experience. They felt acutely aware of the brief and fragmentary nature of this experience and saw too how difficult it was to generalise from it and build on it using the comments of the others. The fact that at one point one of them arrived at the correct answer did not resolve the problem because the answer that was suggested did not seem to fit the perceptions that each had and had verbalised. Looking back at the transcript and analysing the event, none saw this as a lost opportunity or were puzzled that they had passed it by because each was overwhelmed by the experience of searching for agreement when it appeared none existed.

We should explain that the illustrative material we have used here comes from a particular context. We have used the experiences of a group of peace studies students, mostly post-graduate, who had the night before returned from a three-day visit to Croatia, where they had seen different aspects of the war up close (this was in June 1993). Some had visited UN soldiers, others refugees, a women's centre and other institutions. We chose to use this exercise at this point in the course because we wanted to explore the different understandings that people can generate from brief encounters. The students were of different nationalities, from the Americas, Europe, Africa and Asia and for all of them English was a second (or third) language. There is then a critical context for looking at this exercise but the outcomes are not dissimilar from those we have encountered on other occasions when we have used the same exercise with university students studying research methods, a conference of drama professionals, an in-service course for headteachers in Estonia or a group of town planners in Australia.

THE POWER OF PERSONAL EXPERIENCE

Every time we have tried this experiment, one of the first things we notice, as people begin to discuss their encounter with the 'mystery object', is the strength of the authority that they derive from their own experience. Although their knowledge of the object is derived from only a very brief contact between the tip of one finger and a very small part of the object, this brief, selective and partial contact looms large as the central element in their grip on reality. Indeed, as they discuss their encounter with the object, this brief sensation seems to expand in their consciousness, becoming stronger in the face of challenges to it.

You find the strength of this authority revealed in the vehement denials people express in the face of perceptions offered by others which clash with their own. Notice that, in the transcript, when someone else makes a suggestion, even a one word description ('hard'), another will immediately counter it without any hesitation ('No, soft!'). The faith that each person has in the undeniability of their own evidence does not seem to be a consequence of their having a position of power in the group, though their ability to bring their own perception to the fore in discussion may be. Although everyone begins from an equivalent initial position in terms of 'how much' information each has, and appears to have equally relevant knowledge to hand, individual roles quickly emerge. Indeed, in discussing the task the roles taken by individuals are often a key topic. One person will attempt to lead the discussion; others will be content to follow. Some will ask questions; others will make claims. Often you will find that there are gender differences in the roles people take or make for themselves. It is in the nature of this task that what we observe the group doing is struggling for some degree of coherence in the face of conflicting evidence. While each individual tries to fit their experience to the descriptions offered by others, they are able to reach only a few points of contact. But although there are points at which they momentarily arrive at a consensus with one other person, these agreements are tenuous and usually last only a few moments. It is in the nature of the task that the next utterance is likely to break this brief consensus, and once broken it appears to be very difficult for those involved to backtrack and replay the discussion so that they can see exactly the cause of disagreement.

With hindsight, the task seems relatively straightforward, but at the time, for those involved, it is more difficult. It is beyond the concentration of most people to stay with the task and, at the same time, stand back from it in order to observe how the group goes about trying to solve it. It seems to be very rare for people to attempt to seek patterns in what has been said (out loud at least), to collect points of consensus, however fragile, and to use them as a basis for solving the problem. The tendency seems to be for the discussion to roll on, for each utterance to be treated serially, and for those involved not to seek to establish and build on points of agreement. This is, of course, very difficult because the agreement will be established only between two people, never between all three. An unstated rule appears to be that points of agreement are only acceptable when all three agree. Points of agreement between two are usually rejected without recognition. One way some people may seek to find an exit from this impasse is by turning from dogmatic assertion ('It is hard', 'It is soft') to suggesting similes and metaphors. These are often offered to the group (marked by a rising intonation to suggest they are being given a tentative status) but it is unusual for them to be picked up and developed by others. The usual pattern seems to be for a suggested metaphor or simile to be countered by reassertion!

As the discussion proceeds pauses will appear, but even after a pause it remains rare for participants to seek to cumulate knowledge or to refer back to earlier statements. Typically the discussion will cycle and recycle, returning to restatements of previous claims. Very rarely does anyone attempt to recapitulate or summarise what has been discussed. (They may do so in their thoughts, but not within the discussion.) The discussion will thus keep returning to restatements of initial perceptions ('It is hard', 'It is soft', 'It is smooth', 'It is rough') which are represented as undeniable and insuperable barriers to agreement.

Normally, after a period of time within which the starting point will be revisited for perhaps the third time, the authority that each invests in their initial perception will begin to fade. Sometimes you can see people searching for a refreshment of that first touch – they will begin referring to the finger tip, touching it with other fingers, gesturing as they search for words. One response to this sense of the decay of the initial stimulus is to request the opportunity to touch the object again.

Some will recognise the problem that the discussants face as very like the problem that social psychologists sometimes call 'cognitive dissonance'. In the original work on this topic by Leon Festinger *et al.* (1964), which is unusual in its attempts to bring together experimental psychology and social observation, the research problem was that of investigating how people react when what seem to be equally valid pieces of evidence are inconsistent with one another. As well as devising laboratory tests to investigate perceptual dissonance, Festinger also looked to historical situations in which dissonance appeared on a social scale. For example, he looked to millennial cults, such as those in the early Middle Ages, which predicted that the world would end (usually during the year AD 1000), to see how people reacted when such prophecies failed. He also drew parallels to the origins of Christianity, when the disciples having believed Jesus was immortal were faced with the fact of his execution and death. While engaged in this research, Festinger and his colleagues covertly joined a flying saucer cult in Chicago which was making predictions about the world shortly coming to an end, in order to investigate the problem in a 'real life' situation. They reported their studies in a celebrated book, *When Prophecy Fails*, a book which also seems to have been the model for Alison Lurie's novel, *Imaginary Friends*.

The early part of the discussion about the mystery object can be seen as essentially a cognitive mapping exercise involving the location of your own perceptions in a cognitive space: a space that includes the perceptions of others, which must be accommodated. What becomes clear in later discussion – once those involved 'know' the object – is that each has a partial view, an experience of just one aspect of a multi-faceted object from which they have attempted to extrapolate to define the whole object. In retrospect the barrier to agreement seems to be that each was so wedded to the undeniable authority of their initial perception that they were unable to suspend their belief in it for long enough to attempt to find ways of including the perceptions of others.

Universally, it seems, we suspect the accounts of others when they conflict with what we know, assuming them to be mistaken, misguided or in error. We seem to find it more difficult than we expect, or would like to believe, to set aside our own perceptions in order to attend to the reported perceptions of others and, temporarily at least, to grant them equal validity. It is as though we can understand what others see only *through* the lenses of our own understanding. Though in making this claim we are acutely aware that this is a process that can easily be scaled up to describe family, work and teaching situations, and indeed that we may be in danger of replicating the same error in making just this claim!

INSIDE/OUTSIDE

In the way we have been discussing the 'Apple Incident' we have found ourselves falling into a narrative pattern which will be familiar to those who have read or written much social science research. Look back over what we have written in the last few pages. Who is telling the story? Whose voice has assumed authority in giving the account? Is it yours? That of the author/s? The students?

Given the conventions of textbook writing and scientific reporting, you might expect that the narrative 'voice' in the account we have given is that of the objective observer – the notional outsider who has tried to watch closely what happens without becoming directly involved. As authors we used direct quotations from others at the start but as the discussion/

Illustration 5 Elephant sculpture cartoon (the late Albert Saunders)
Source: Container Marketing Ltd

analysis of the incident proceeds, the narrative moves away from recall of the incident towards an interpretation that is more general and seemingly more theoretical, returning only occasionally to the transcript as a way of renewing touch with it. By this point in the text, the narrative voice is clearly and solely that of the authors. In this move from description to interpretation, the 'I' or the 'us' in the experiment, who feature so strongly at the start, have become 'them'. We believe that this is not incidental, and not just a rhetorical device, but touches on central questions about the nature of the social relationships that constitute social research.

The exercise demonstrates in a graphic, even a dramatic, way that social research inevitably involves the negotiation of meaning among the people involved. As those who are trying to identify the mystery object discuss what happened with those who were witnesses to the event, it becomes clear that the 'object' being discussed is not so much the apple as the interaction itself. The sub-text of the discussion becomes the process by which those involved attempt to reach a resolution of the problem they face in negotiating their different perceptions. As the discussion proceeds, what the apple 'means' comes to be found less in recourse to the stock of knowledge (about apples) located in common sense and everyday language and more and more in the problematic nature of social interaction.

The assumption that we normally make about the nature of social research is that it is a systematic activity intended to create authoritative knowledge about an object, a group of objects, a situation, a location, a group of people, or perhaps a series of events, or some combination of all these things. This knowledge gains its authority in part from its source as a product of tested methods and in part from its argued relation to the accumulated and accepted generalisations, arguments and concepts which we refer to as theory. The claims of research are that it creates knowledge of a kind that is grounded in objective measures of the real world and transmuted through theory so that those outside the immediate setting will recognise similar or parallel situations in which they are involved or have at hand. Further we assume that access to and understanding of the limitations of research-based knowledge will allow others to act more effectively within the scope and confines of their own practice.

We can summarise the central relationships between the subject of research, those who do the research and those who receive or make use of it in a diagram (see Figure 1).

Notice that there is some intentional ambiguity here. 'I/us' can be the researcher or the research team, or we can be the receivers and users of research. Similarly 'you/them' can be the subjects of research and 'it' the research report or the product of research. For the moment though, let us discuss these relationships as though 'I/we' were the researchers, 'you/them' the audience and 'it' the object being researched. Given this perspective, initially we tend to see the essential research problem as one of 'I/us' forming an unambiguous and objective description of 'it', such that subjective overtones are minimised and what we have is a definitive, discrete and specific definition of the object that anyone will recognise without confusion.

This seems to be the way in which those who observed our three blind researchers first conceptualised the problem. The task was seen as a problem-solving exercise, in which the research team tried to locate a meaning for the three contrasting perceptions which resolved perceptual dissonance and incongruity. (Though you may be interested to note that

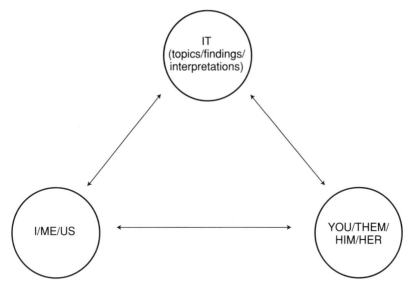

Figure 1 Relationships in research

when they hit on the correct solution – 'It's an apple' – they rejected it because, while it was correct, it did not seem right.) In the negotiation of meanings between the researchers it quickly became clear that this is not quite the systematic process that research textbooks would mostly have us believe. Some members of the research group argue more forcefully than others, some are more tenacious when their ideas or their perceptions are challenged. Very rarely will the research team pause to consider their strategy and to question its effectiveness. Typically women follow and mediate rather than initiate and insist (though we hasten to add we intend this as an observation of sexism, not as a sexist observation).

Inevitably, research is a social process. Not all researchers will need to manage group processes of the kind we have suggested but they will have to negotiate with sponsors, colleagues, and a wide and increasing array of institutions and organisations (ethics committees, granting bodies, academic supervisors, colleagues, peers, the press, politicians and the accumulated arguments that are to be found in the research literature). As each of these audiences will have different information requirements, so the research will show them each a slightly different facet of the research according to their questions, interests and concerns. In our diagram perhaps we should change the circles and replace them by cut diamonds, able to show a different facet as they are turned to different attitudes and directions.

One of the key difficulties we face in trying to develop research as a means of social transformation is that of taking a process out of one social context and reconstructing it in another. In attempting to devise and encourage small-scale and local research that starts from a position of respecting the perceptions that others bring to the research, we inevitably confront contradiction. Encouraging people to express their perceptions, understandings and feelings about real social situations may exacerbate false consciousness in the sense that Brian Fay describes this as 'a set of interrelated illusions about human needs and about how one should act in one's relations with others to achieve certain of these things' (Fay 1977: 214).

Fay argues that when people have to give up the practices which they have acquired from experience and which they have learnt to feel happy about, then they face difficulties. He thinks it is extremely difficult to change social practices on the practical level, 'because giving up such illusions requires abandoning one's self-conceptions and the social practices that they engender and support, things people cling to because they provide direction and meaning in their lives. It involves acquiring a new self-identity' (Fay 1977: 214). The paradox is that research that starts from a position of treating people's perceptions and feelings seriously may find itself creating situations in which these same perceptions and feelings are put under threat of erasure.

Just how illusion is framed is more fragile than Fay appears to admit, though it seems true that 'seeing' an elephant or an apple, when you have built your life (even for a few minutes) around the assumption that it is something else, can be a challenging experience. 'Seeing anew' the school in which you teach, the class in which you are studying, the place in which you work, your family, community, gender, race or class can be transformative in ways that defy the immediate prediction of outcomes.

3 Collective memory-work: the self as a re/source for re/search

With Barbara Schratz-Hadwich

> The critical ontology of ourselves has to be considered . . . as an attitude, an ethos, a philosophical life in which the critique of what we are is at one and the same time the historical analysis of the limits that are imposed on us and an experiment in going beyond them.
>
> (Foucault 1984: 50)

'Memory-work' is a new and distinctive method of social research developed by a group of feminist researchers and scholars, mostly from Berlin, who were involved with the student movement in the 1960s, who have been members of various women's socialist groups and have worked as academics and professionals in teaching and in social science. More recently the methods of memory-work have been used elsewhere, often for different purposes and with different intentions, but the original group comprised women who found themselves increasingly alienated from research, feeling that the process of creating research 'products' left them disconnected from the research process, both as researchers and, even more, as research subjects. They were dissatisfied with the divorce of theory from everyday experience as well as concerned that the individualistic approach of most research had the effect of undermining the capacity for collective action that they had learned from their experiences in women's groups. Their experiences of research thus echoed many of their other experiences as women in a patriarchal social world.

While this chapter is concerned mainly with memory-work as a research method, Frigga Haug (1990) points out that the gaps left by patriarchal research are not only in method but also in content. For instance, while psychology deals extensively with fears of death (particularly psychoanalysis where this is a predominant theme), in all her work with women on the topic of 'fear', fear of death has never been mentioned, so it seems that this particular (male) fear has come to dominate our understanding of fear more generally. One response to the criticism this implies could be to identify these gaps and seek to close them but this response is inadequate, for the power differentials between men and women characterise research at every turn. Recognising this, the Berlin Group turned its attention to reconstructing social science research by first analysing its own implicit patterns of power and authority. The search was for a methodology which would bridge the gap between the subjects and the objects of research and would make research itself a collective process (cf. Projekt Frauengrundstudium 1982, Haug *et al.* 1983, 1987 and Haug 1990). The starting point was to challenge accepted notions of objectivity by disrupting the conventional separation of the researcher from the researched, using personal experience as a basis of social knowledge. This move was premised on an insight that had been developed in women's groups in which they had been involved, that women's identities are not only a consequence of social structures but also a response to them. They were acutely aware that women actively participate or collude in the formation and adoption of the same identities from which they may seek to escape or want to resist:

> The very notion that our own past experience may offer some insight into the ways in which individuals construct themselves into existing relations, thereby themselves reproducing a social formation, itself contains an implicit argument for a particular methodology. If we refuse to understand ourselves simply as a bundle of reactions to all-powerful structures, or to the social relations within which we have formed us, if we search instead for possible indications of how we have participated actively in the formation of our own past experience, then the usual mode of social-scientific research, in which individuals figure exclusively as objects of the process of research, has to be abandoned. For too long, empirical research has approached human beings from the point of view of their controllability, the predictability of their actions. Character traits and modes of behaviours have thus been catalogued as fixed elements within human subjectivity. Since, however, we are concerned here with the possible means whereby human beings may themselves assume control, and thus with the potential prospect of liberation, our research itself must be seen as an intervention into existing practices. . . . Indeed memory-work is only possible if the subject and the object are one and the same.
>
> (Haug 1987: 34–5)

Having established the need to deconstruct the researcher/subject distinction, the Berlin Group began working on memories. Why begin with memories? At first sight memories appear to be at the extreme of what is personal and individual, where we might expect to find the balance tipped firmly towards socialisation and away from emancipation. For most people, memories, especially early memories, mark those options for the expansion and liberation of the self that we feel we have lost. Yet by taking what appeared to be a difficult case in terms of their search for a method that required the critical reconstitution of individualism, the first 'memory-workers' began, first to unravel, and then to challenge this (psychoanalytic) assumption of early experience as a prison of the self.

Memory-work accepts the view that anything a person remembers constitutes a relevant trace in his or her construction of self. Memories, it is assumed, are not direct quotations from experience, but are continually reprocessed in the formation of identity, a process in which certain events from the past acquire subjective significance. What is significant about memories is not their surface validity as true records, but their active role in the construction of identity. The task for memory-work is to reveal the processes by which we construct our sense of self by uncovering successive layers of significance in personal accounts.

Memory-workers claim that the work they do is research, not therapy; memories may play a role in memory-work that is comparable to the role that dreams play in psychoanalysis, but the allusion to psychoanalysis is misleading. Memory-work is not intended as a therapy, nor is its primary concern with self-knowledge. It is concerned to close the gaps between theory and experience in ways that are intended to change the nature of experience, not simply to accept it. It is, therefore, more focused on political and social action than we might have led you to believe in the way we have described it. The key to the critical distinction between memory-work and psychoanalysis begins in the concept, derived from George Herbert Mead, of a duality within the self altogether different from Freudian conceptions of the individual psyche:

> What perhaps is not so familiar or obvious is that the relation between oneself and one's memories of one's past experience is similar to the relation between other agents and oneself. One's self engages with one's memories, has a conversation with them, responds to them, as another responds to oneself. Memories are essential to the duality of self. The 'I' reflects back on the 'me' and together they constitute the self. Memories contain the traces of the continuing process of appropriation of the social and the becoming, the constructing, of self.
>
> (Crawford *et al.* 1992: 39)

But always in memory-work there is a tension arising from the duality between the role that memory, and memories, play in socialisation and social control and the persistent potential that they have to undermine them:

> In their attempt to wrest meaning from the world, persons construct themselves; and in their struggle for intelligibility they reflect. They remember the problematic, which is itself socially produced, in terms

of the resolution previously sought if not achieved. Memory-work thus
is intimately bound up with the uncovering of the processes of the
construction of self.

(Crawford *et al.* 1992: 39)

The act of remembering actions, episodes and events from the past
makes certain aspects of the process of identity-forming accessible. It
also reopens earlier negotiations between the 'I' and the 'me', sometimes
creating powerful voices in the transformation of the individual self as
conceived within a particular social context.

In Figure 2 we have tried to show how we are not only passively caught
in the socialisation process but carry within us the potential to transform
our lives. Within each aspect of identity there are the traces of both
oppression and a potential for resistance, which are difficult to separate
in everyday actions. Memory-work can be used to expose earlier understandings we have of ourselves and of each other in the light of current
understandings in ways that may explain the underlying conditions of the
processes involved. The key question for memory-work is not, who am I?
But, how did we get to be the way we are and how can we change?

What is at stake in memory-work is the nature of the demarcation
between what is felt and seen to be personal, and what is identified as
social. Frigga Haug (1990) talks of a distinction between 'person' and
'personality', arguing that what belongs to the 'person' should remain
undisclosed in memory-work and that the focus should be on the 'personality', that is to say those aspects of the self that are socially constructed.
Some years ago the social anthropologist Ward Goodenough drew a similar
distinction between personal and social identities, not in terms of our self-
perception of ourselves as individual, but in terms of the consequences that
different facets of our identity have for others:

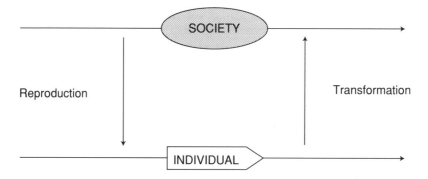

Figure 2 From reproduction to transformation

A social identity is an aspect of self that makes a difference in how one's rights and duties distribute to specific others. Any aspect of self whose alteration entails no change in how people's rights and duties are mutually distributed, although it affects their emotional orientations to one another and the way they choose to exercise their privileges, has to do with personal identity not with social identity.

(Goodenough 1965: 4–5)

In part, what memory-work does is to force a reconceptualisation of this distinction, and its implied notion of privacy, in which much of what is conventionally taken to be personal is made social. The rights and duties that Goodenough identified in Trukese village communities have to be reassessed when we consider life in contemporary Europe, and elsewhere. Apparently enduring social structures such as those provided by the family, the community, the Church, the political boundaries of the state as well as what counts as violence, or unacceptable transgressions of individual rights, are reassessed and made provisional at a number of levels but nowhere less than in the immediate social relations between people. The line between what is personal and what is social becomes blurred and the distinction becomes redundant. The ways in which people interrelate, their expectations of their relationships with one another and the styles and manners of their interaction, whether actual or virtual, destabilise the taken-for-granted notion of the personal and social being insulated one from the other. The 'roles', and therefore the actions, of men and women, family members, teachers, employees, strangers, children, everyone in every circumstance are apparently becoming increasingly unpredictable and indeterminate. Consequently we are continually thrown back on our own moral resources in order to know what to do and how to react in the face of the unexpected, and in this process 'emotion' cannot be restricted to our private lives since it is also an aspect of what is social.

Within memory-work there is a continual underlying conflict between the radical and the conservative, between memories of the past, inevitably tinged with a degree of nostalgia, and a need to find in this past keys to the locks that constrain our actions, and our sense of self, in the present. The exploratory work of Frigga Haug and her collaborators led them to the method of starting from their *writing of stories* about situations or events which they had experienced in the course of their lives. These are not stories of trauma and crisis but stories of everyday experience, episodes or accounts like those we all remember from our own life histories. From this starting point Frigga Haug argues that it is important to *work historically* if we want to find out the social construction, the mechanisms, connections and meanings of our actions and feelings.

In developing the method, turning to the writing of personal stories about everyday events appears to invite the very romanticised individual perspective on autobiographical reconstruction from which the group sought an escape. To turn full face into the problem rather than turning away from it was an unusually brilliant move! It became crucial, though, to ensure that memories of everyday life were not seen through an individual perspective but rendered in a form that encouraged a different form of analysis. As a first step, the group chose to *work collectively* on their written sketches. The emphasis is equally emphatic on each word; *collective, memory* and *work*. For Haug the result is a necessary, enjoyable, new, important social research methodology (Haug 1990: 47).

For those who are unfamiliar with collective memory-work, it is not possible to describe it fully here, instead we will give an idea of how we have used it in the context of problems that are somewhat different from those faced by the originators of the approach. If you want to try the method yourself we advise you first to read the books by Haug and Crawford and their collaborators from which we have quoted here and, if possible, take part in one of the workshops they run.

THE PROCESS OF COLLECTIVE MEMORY-WORK

Over the years, Frigga Haug and her colleagues have developed a set of procedures for collective memory-work which are best treated as a set of rules. Some of the rules might seem strange or unnecessary at first but they have been shown to work in practice and they have survived significant tests of experience. The rules for memory-work we outline here are derived from Haug *et al.* (1987) and Crawford *et al.* (1992) (see Figure 3).

In the first phase, as in any research work, the starting point is to find adequate research questions for the memory-work to follow. In memory-work, no less than in any other form of research, the substantive content of the research is of critical importance and the way in which the problem is framed, while it will keep changing, determines much of what follows. Memory-work, however, does not build on the insights, predilections or obsessions of a single researcher. In the first phase, all co-researchers, that is everybody taking part in the research group(s), should be involved in deciding on the themes and topics to be followed. It is important to note here that memory-work groups are usually self-selected groups of people who want to work together and have some sympathy for the ideas that inform the methods. Introducing memory-work to a heterogeneous and diverse university class faced with assessment is a quite different proposition. This does not mean it cannot be done, but it should be done with thought.

Once a theme has been agreed, in small groups of four to five, each member/researcher writes a memory which relates to the chosen theme. This memory is usually of an everyday, but particular episode, event or

2 Group meets and analyses
each written memory.

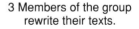

1 Each member of the group writes
a memory.

3 Members of the group
rewrite their texts.

4 Analyses of the texts are
related to other theories.

Figure 3 Phases in the memory-work process

action from their experience. The text is always written in the third person, which may initially seem strange but distances the actor in the event from the person who remembers the experience. The written text should illuminate the scene(s) in as much detail as possible, including even inconsequential or trivial detail, but without offering any interpretation or explanation for what is described. The process will work better if participants write about one of their earliest memories rather than something recent. Usually people will write one to several pages, depending on how long they are given to do so; ideally they should be given several days. Sometimes, for workshop purposes, we have had people write in 30 minutes or so, but this should be avoided if at all possible. One of the most interesting parts of the process for participants is that the moments they choose to write about rarely pop straight into their heads but come to them only after several days of thinking around the theme. This process, in which memories are searched, examined and refiled before one is selected for close scrutiny, is not wasted time since reflection on the process of memory selection will later feed deliberation and discussion.

In the second phase, the texts are exchanged and analysed by the group. It is important to emphasise that this process is very different from that used by conventional discussion groups organised around the reading of a text, even though memory-work groups often evolve from reading groups. Since interpretation does not figure in the text, and since the author has anyway adopted the convention of writing in the third person, there is little

1 Problem of the author

2 What introduces the author as . . . . (the topic):

Author's activities	Author's interests, wishes	Author's feelings
Other persons and their activities	Other persons' interests and wishes	Other persons' feelings

Blind spots (what is missing)	Language (clichés, construction of language active/passive, etc.)	Connection of persons/ situations	Contradictions

3 Construction of the author's self	Construction of the other persons

4 Problem lying underneath the scene

Compared to other theories

Figure 4 Memory-work worksheet
Source: Frigga Haug

heed given to stylistics or to literary or expressive form. In addition, the conventional authority of the 'author' in relation to the reader hardly figures at all. By analysing each others' memory texts all authors become co-researchers and as such each becomes part of the research process, acting both as subject and object in a process of knowledge production.

Analysis of the text proceeds by stages; initially, each memory-work group member expresses opinions and ideas about one memory with which the group chooses to start. In doing this they are encouraged to work on the task of identifying the actors' motives and other aspects of the memory which lie between the lines of the text, that is the search is for possible meanings which have not been directly expressed by the author. Using the worksheet (Figure 4), which Frigga Haug has developed for use in workshops on memory-work, helps keep the discussion disciplined. Initially it is tempting to ask the author to adjudicate when there are differences of interpretation. ('What did you mean when you wrote . . .?') This is to be avoided! The text should be treated as a text, not a testimony and interpretation is not as useful as exploring the way that language is used. It must be emphasised that this is often a slow process. Analysing a one-page text will usually take a group from three to six hours, and in some instances much longer. As the discussion proceeds new ideas will emerge as understanding accumulates but for this to happen patience and disciplined attention to the text is required.

Haug and Crawford both suggest that it may be helpful to identify clichés, generalisations, contradictions, cultural imperatives, metaphor, etc., and to discuss 'practical theories', popular conceptions, sayings and images about the topic in the specific text. We have found metaphor particularly productive, not just in identifying metaphors within the text but in having the group develop the practice of using their own metaphors to understand it. Especially with a new group which is carefully feeling its way with the process, it is often useful to ask, 'What does this remind you of? What pictures come to mind?' This might seem to contradict what we said about disciplined attention to the text but we meant this not in the sense it might be intended in literary criticism but in trying to identify meanings. The criteria for the analysis of the collected texts are the relevant traces of the social formation process, which are often to be found in gaps and in silences or in the clichés and contradictions contained within the collected written texts. Thus the researchers ask each other (not necessarily the author) for clarification of ambiguities, for more background information on what is missing and the social role(s) of the actor(s) involved.

After analysing each individual memory text the group looks for similarities and differences between the memories and looks for continuous elements among memories whose relation to each other is not immediately apparent. The group looks to question aspects of the memories which do not appear to fit. In this process the layers of meaning accumulate in a way that is very difficult to describe in a linear text. Meaning comes to depend on membership, presence and witness. Australian Aboriginal people say that to miss an important event, particularly a funeral, is to allow a part of the community to die. They may not continue for 40,000 years but there is something of this sense about memory-work groups as they come to share access to, and ownership of, an area of shared knowledge. Like families, or groups who work closely together, they come to share a common history, a common culture, which depends on presence and cannot be shared with others just by telling them about it.

In the next phase, the members of the group rewrite their original memory texts, paying particular attention to the questions raised by their co-researchers in the analytical phase. By modifying the texts, the authors engage in a reflexive process which brings to light new 'data' from their memory. These memories might have been suppressed and may suggest starting points for the reinterpretation of the construction of self.

The new memory texts are discussed again among the co-researchers. This time the original versions of the memories are compared and contrasted with the second ones and examined further, and common themes are discussed in view of a new understanding of the overall topic. If there are other memory-work groups involved, the findings and discussions are exchanged across the groups. This process of collective theorising is a powerful feature of memory-work and often involves relating to other theoretical positions and other kinds of research.

THE USES OF COLLECTIVE MEMORY-WORK

Memory-work has so far been mainly developed and used in the investigation of feminist topics, like female sexualisation (Haug *et al.* 1987) or emotions and gender (Crawford *et al.* 1992). It has also been used in a more directly applied form by Susan Kippax (one of the co-authors of the Crawford book) in the investigation of the memories men and women (hetero- and homosexual) have of sexual contact as part of a project in HIV/AIDS research (Kippax *et al.* 1990) and by Lindsay Fitzclarence (1991b) as a way of helping student teachers understand the nature of authority as they attempt to manage the difficult transition between the roles of student and teacher. In our own work we have successfully used it with students in a course on intercultural learning and in a research methodology course in a peace studies programme.

In a conventional book it is not possible to reproduce the sometimes exciting and stimulating life of a memory-work group. Nevertheless, we will try to convey some of our experience of this work by giving an example of a memory story, its discussion and its final revision. It is taken from a course for university students dealing with the difficulties of living together in culturally diverse groups (see Fuchs and Schratz 1994). The aim was to use memory-work to help students develop an understanding of their own racism in an everyday and institutional setting.

In a first step, the whole group brain-stormed the topic of racism, and, after considerable discussion, agreed on a theme that served as a starting point for small memory-work groups, each consisting of four to six co-researchers. Like Haug and Crawford, we found it was important to make this choice of theme collectively. Since memory-work is confronted by the problem of the uniqueness or singularity of any given experience, a collective decision ensures a commitment to generalisability. If people share a commitment to the theme, then each memory the group generates becomes a valid source of reference within the later discussions of the group. Frigga Haug writes:

> Since it is as individuals that we interpret and suffer our lives, our experiences appear unique and thus of no value for scientific analysis. The mass character of social processes is obliterated within the concept of individuality. Yet we believe that the notion of the uniqueness of experience and of the various ways in which it is consciously assessed is a fiction. The number of possibilities for action open to us is radically limited. We live according to a whole series of imperatives: social pressures, natural limitations, the imperative of economic survival, the given conditions of history and culture. Human beings produce their lives collectively. It is within the domain of collective production that individual experience becomes possible. If therefore a given experience is possible, it is also subject to universalization. What we perceive as 'personal' ways of adapting to the social are also potentially generalizable modes of appropriation. Using our experience – in a positive as well as a negative sense – as an empirical base for our work thus offered the possibility of studying each individual mode of appropriation in detail. Our work derived its impetus from our recognition of the human potential to expand a capacity for action, to develop new possibilities, to enjoy diverse sensual pleasures; this was what led us to investigate the conditions of production of these pleasures, and to press for their universalization. Equally, we considered it vitally important to recognize recurrent forms of suffering in their specificity, in order to avoid reproducing them in the future.
>
> (Haug *et al.* 1987: 43–4)

In view of these considerations we decided on themes which were open both to actual individual experiences and to generalisable conclusions for intercultural learning. One of the themes chosen was that of encountering someone with another skin colour, a theme to which everybody could contribute. Moreover, this theme seemed important because we all knew and understood the importance of external appearance and the role that skin colour plays in racism.

In what follows, we first present the first version of one memory story, then a summary of the discussions in the memory-work group and finally the revised, second version of the memory text.

Encountering someone of another colour (first version)

'As often on his long journey around the United States he was waiting at a filthy Greyhound bus station for the bus to arrive . He used to spend most of the day sightseeing and tried to sleep on the bus while getting to the following destination. Otherwise he would not have been able to cover the long distances on his trip, and by doing so, he saved accommodation expenses. His journey had taken him from Washington D.C., where he had worked as an au-pair boy for six weeks, up north along the East Coast, right across Canada to the West Coast, south along the West Coast and across the States back East again. He always used to choose routes which took him to the well-known sights of the respective areas. This time he was travelling south in the State of Mississippi to meet an American he had gotten to know during his stay in the US.

'This area left a poorer impression with him than the other places he had seen so far. He could not see any tourists around there, there were mainly exclusively poor people who seemed to live there. Nevertheless, waiting at the bus station there was not much different from having done it anywhere else. He was surrounded by rather poor people who could only afford the bus as the cheapest means of transport. Among them there were lots of homeless who could be found in the country of unlimited opportunities in the same way as in any other country. For them the bus station seemed to be the meeting place as it is the case with train stations in European countries. He only stuck out of the local people because of his mountain rucksack, which rendered him the character of a rambler. Moreover, in this area of the US also being caucasian was rather the exception so that he stood out even more from the group of people waiting for the buses.

'After the bus had arrived and the passengers had boarded, the usual Greyhound ritual started: the driver walks through the rows of seats and checks the tickets, then he announces on the loudspeaker: "This is a non-smoking . . .". He had found a seat in the rear third of the bus and prepared himself for a longer trip across the State. Slowly he realised that he was the only white person on the bus. It was the first time this had happened to him during his trip. To make sure his impression was right he looked back and eventually took it for sure. The other passengers did not take any notice of him, while he started becoming aware of the unusual situation. He looked at the different physiognomy in the form of the black people's heads and was reminded of the figure of the "Little Black Nigger Boy" which had been standing on the primary school teacher's desk for the purpose of collecting money for missionary activities by the Church when he first went to school. Every time somebody put in a coin, the "Nigger Boy" would nod.

'When he was watching the black passengers on the bus, however, he did not have that neat perception any more. On the contrary, some heads seemed quite clumsy, almost threatening, although he only saw them from behind. After some time he started noticing a strange smell in the bus, which reminded him of a particular spice which he had come across for the first time when he was invited for lunch by a black family on his trip. It was not a pleasant smell; in its intensity he found it quite penetrating. Is it sweat or mouth odour, he wondered? On his journey, he had always got some packed lunch with him, but the strange smell did not let his appetite arise. He would rather not eat anything this time until he got to the next stop. Instead, some passengers started opening their own lunch packets and began eating the food in a noisy way. He then noticed the strange smell of that spice even more intensively in the bus. (Even nowadays, many years after, he can identify the former smell and associates it with negative feelings.)

'He also had always something to read with him in order to bridge the travelling time if he was not able to sleep on the bus. This time he had not even succeeded in doing some reading on this trip. Next to him sat a black woman with a voluminous body. She needed more than just her own seat and her buttocks reached over onto his seat. He was slim and therefore had enough room, but he rather lent towards the aisle, in order to avoid too close a body contact. Generally, he quite liked body contact, but in this particular situation he did not feel like it. The more so as the woman had meanwhile unpacked her knitting-needles and, apparently without paying attention to her seat neighbour, had begun moving her left needle up and down in rough movements in front of his body. He tried to lean towards the aisle even more so as not to be accidentally hit by the needle. She did not seem to pay any attention to him.

'When it started dawning outside a strange feeling overcame him. He did not know whether it was fear or simply a dull feeling of strangeness: for the first time he completely felt being in the minority. And although he had regarded himself as a very tolerant person, he caught himself in thoughts like "What happens if . . .?" He felt not only disturbed by the penetrant smell but also by the sight that the black passengers also simply threw their rubbish on the floor. Then he eventually fell asleep. He was happy when he had reached the destination, where he was met by the white peanut farmer whom he had met previously on his journey through the States. For the first time he felt belonging to somebody of the same colour of the skin.'

DISCUSSION OF THE MEMORY TEXT

The memory story above was actively and extensively discussed by the co-researchers in the memory-work group. It is only possible to reproduce a short summary of the discussion here. In order to differentiate the discussion in the group from the memory story we have chosen the present tense for its reproduction. The plural forms of the personal pronoun ('we', 'us', 'our') are used to stress the importance of the collective work among the co-researchers in the group.

The person is described as a person travelling extensively, which means he does not really have an interest in staying long enough in one place to be confronted by its particular culture. Therefore, real intercultural encounters do not often take place for the traveller, even though here the narrator gets into close contact with the local people on the bus. In our memory group we talk about the German saying '*Reisen bildet*' [travelling educates], since the writer legitimises his journey as an educational trip: He had first worked as an '*au-pair boy*' in order to visit the '*well-known sights*'. We asked if travelling had not hardened the prejudices the person had already. Otherwise the sights would not have been worth the visit and so well known that he could plan his routes accordingly.

Travelling as a tourist always means being outside the places you visit. The tourist can come and go when he or she pleases, a freedom which separates the visitor from the local inhabitants. Although in the scene described the writer experiences being in the minority, as a tourist he is a person who is free to move. We asked him how old he was at the time of the story. He was a student in the Tyrol at that time, which also explains his *mountain* rucksack, which made him distinct, not only from the local people waiting there but also from other travellers.

Differentiating himself from others is a theme that runs through the whole text like a thread. The white colour of his skin makes him aware of his minority position on the bus and affects his feelings. ('*Generally, he quite liked body contact, but in this particular situation he did not feel like it.*') The very nature of environment seemed to change, the writer says that the places he had visited before seemed to be less poor and therefore more frequented by tourists, whereas here he found '*mainly people who seemed to live there*', '*rather poor people who could only afford the bus as the cheapest means of transport*' and '*among them there were lots of homeless*'. Richer areas, we assumed, are rather more frequented by white people than this area, where '*his white colour of the skin was rather the exception*'. He further demarcates himself from the people around him by describing how far he had already travelled and by high-lighting the differences which make him distinct from the others '*so that he stood out*'.

We noticed that in the story it is the main actor, the white tourist, who shows 'active' interests. We experience him as an au-pair boy (we wanted to know how a male student gets a summer job of that kind), as a culturally interested and intellectual person and somebody who reads, whereas the African Americans on the bus have attributed to them rather depreciative qualities. Like the homeless at European train stations, they meet at the bus station, on the bus they eat in a way that does not stimulate his appetite, and the woman next to him knits '*in rough movements*' and prevents him from falling asleep.

The example of the knitting woman showed further divisions between the people who are referred to, this time hierarchically. The (higher) level of the intellectual (*reading*) as opposed to the (lower) level of the technical and manual (*knitting*), the person of white skin as opposed to black, the male as opposed to the female. There is also the demarcation marked by smell, which has a high emotional impact on the writer. Incidentally, he mentioned in the discussion group that usually he was not so sensitive to smell. Since he could not withdraw from it on the bus, he experienced it as repulsive: '*It was not a pleasant smell; in its intensity he found it quite penetrating. . . . Even nowadays, many years after, he can identify the former smell and associates it with negative feelings.*'

We were struck that the narrator associates this unpleasant smell, which he attributes to a particular spice, with excretions of the body (sweat or mouth odour). Associations with food and the body exist within a binary opposition (clean/dirty) within which strong and barely controlled emotions are usually invested and implicitly associated with moral judgements. In cultures in which hygiene and training in cleanliness are highly valued (like Austria) smells are vigorously hidden away or avoided. Therefore dirt, smells and noise can generate strong feelings when people from different cultures live together.

The narrator loses his appetite because of the '*eating noises*' and '*the penetrating smells*', which he experiences as unpleasant and threatening. How strongly those impressions have been imprinted in his subconsciousness shows in the passage that '*Even nowadays, many years after, he can identify the former smell and associates it with negative feelings*'. In a similar way he feels threatened by the close contact of the '*voluminous body*' of the black woman sitting next to him with '*her buttocks*' reaching over to his seat. One member of the memory group thinks of the image of the fat black woman in movies who is depicted as the 'good mammy' rather than as a threatening person from whom one withdraws. We did not venture further as this seems to touch the boundary between memory-work (involving the personality) and therapy (involving the person) to which Frigga Haug refers. Nevertheless, we came to the conclusion that questions of body contact, eroticism and sexuality seem to play an important part in intercultural encounters and we looked at this in another series of memory texts in our work which we have not included here.

It also interested us that the narrator not only experiences the black woman's body as threatening but that he also presents the needle as a kind of 'weapon' with which he could be hit, even if by accident. Somebody also pointed out that, from a feminist perspective, knitting as a skill and as a means of female productivity could also be seen as an instrument of domination over men. The only thing he can hold against her is his escape into an intellectual act because he '*had always something to read*'. It is interesting that in the second version the narrator was '*taking out a book and holding it demonstratively in front of his head when reading it*' (as a weapon of defence?) so that he '*could at least get her to narrow the radius of the movements of the needles*'. In the first version he tries to escape this '*threat*' by moving his body from her towards the aisle of the bus '*so as not to be accidentally hit by the needle*'.

When asked about the contradiction in the different reactions in the two versions the writer explained that he had at first tried to turn away from her, as described in the first version. After some time he used the book, as described in the second version, otherwise he would have had to remain with his body in an awkward position. What was striking in our discussion was the common trait in both versions that intercultural communication between the people or cultures did not really take place. We are confronted with avoidance rather than communication.

Regarding the contrast between the '*black woman with a voluminous body*' and the emphasis on the intellectual capacities of the 'slim white man', we asked whether the narrator had been influenced in his perception by ethnocentrally desirable beauty ideals. For Wolf (1990: 12):

> 'Beauty' is a currency system like the gold standard. Like any economy, it is determined by politics, and in the modern age in the West it is the last, best belief system that keeps male dominance intact. In assigning value to women in a vertical hierarchy according to a culturally imposed physical standard, it is an expression of power relations in which women must unnaturally compete for resources that men have appropriated for themselves.

The man seemed to have difficulties in making contact with the black woman although he spoke English. This was a period when fashion models were all slim, young and white and the memory-work group suggested that he would not have had any problems if a young, slim (white) woman had sat next to him.

We got a similar impression when discussing the writer's description of the other '*black*' people on the bus. For the narrator they appear only shadowy and threatening as is indicated in the sentence: '*some heads seemed quite clumsy, almost threatening, although he only saw them from behind*'. We started discussing the important part that the shape of the head played in the theory of race. Phrenology (the scientific study of the headform) was a decisive force in the emergence and dissemination of the idea of racism (cf. Miles 1989). We asked if the passengers on the bus did not have any other characteristics and traits which attracted the narrator's attention and asked some other questions like 'Was there no contact or conversation at all between him and the others?' 'Was there not even any kind of eye contact?'

In contrast to the description of the black passengers on the bus is the '*Little Black Nigger Boy*', who represents his first encounter with black people. Compared to the people on the bus that figure was '*neat*' and unthreatening. However, even then there was no intercultural communication with the 'child' from the foreign culture but only a mechanical nod, thanking you for your gift to the missionaries. The situation on the bus is characterised by the same lack of speech and creates another demarcation between the narrator and the other passengers. We do not know from the text, however, whether the latter had communicated with each other at all. The only expression of language appears in the announcement of the bus driver by means of one-way communication, apart from that language is absent. It was interesting to notice that in other texts too, missing or interrupted verbal communication played an important part. In no case was this a matter of language barriers but always a problem of people from different cultures making contact with each other.

We discussed in detail the meaning of the phrase '*And although he had regarded himself as a very tolerant person, he caught himself in thoughts like "What happens if . . . ?"*' This stirred up an intense discussion on the term 'tolerance', we asked questions like 'What lies behind the tolerance of the narrator?' 'Why doesn't he show feelings and emotions?' 'Does he suppress or repress them and by doing so does he think he is being tolerant?' The memory text contains several hints that certain aspects of the passengers' behaviour seem to disturb him but the emotions (aggression) we expected in his own behaviour are faded out or distorted.

Later in the memory-work process, when we talked about general theories of racism we noted that Devereux (1973) argues that distortion is particularly developed where the (research) material under inquiry arouses fear. Researchers who deal with this kind of material seem to safeguard themselves against this fear by either suppressing certain parts of their material or by mitigating, that is not analysing or wrongly interpreting it, but by describing it in an ambiguous way or by arranging it in a new and different way. He further argues that suppression and repression appear when someone is threatened in his or her own identity and leads to fear of the other, of strangeness.

The description of the rising dawn on the bus reminds us of the feelings young children have when they must go to bed. Just as children experience insecurity and anxiety when confronted with night coming, so we interpret the narrator's '*dull feeling of strangeness*', the feeling of being alone or being left alone, as a possible form of regression into (early) childhood. His thought of *'What happens if . . . ?'* reminds us of the 'incendiary compositions' [*BrandSätze*] (Jäger 1992), which ignite racism through verbal phrases like *'Who's afraid of the Black Man?'* which appears in the second version of the text (see below). Whereas in the children's game it is possible to run away, the narrator has to stay on the bus all night. He is only free from fear when he falls asleep, and when he is met by the white farmer, with whom he feels a sense of *'belonging to'* because of his *'colour of the skin'*.

Encountering someone of another colour (second version)

'He was then in his early twenties and had used his university summer holidays to explore the "locations" of his American Studies course. By doing so he, on the one hand, was interested in improving his language competence, on the other hand he wanted to get to know the country and the people. For the first six weeks he had arranged to stay as an au-pair boy with an American family at the West Coast, where he was intensively confronted with the American vernacular. For the second part of his stay he had bought a bus pass on the Greyhound system, which entitled him unlimited travelling around the States and Canada for two months so as to get to know as much as possible about people and country.

'He had already been on his way for a couple of weeks and had got used to the routines doing the sightseeing during the day and sleeping on the bus during the night. Although it was quite tiring it enabled him to cover as many miles as possible and to live on little money. During his trip he was often invited by people he had met on the way to stay with them, which made it possible for him to clean himself properly and recuperate. Once again he was on the way to meet one of the people he had met, a peanut farmer in the South of the US, who had invited him for such a visit.

'After a long journey from the East Coast up north, across Canada to the West Coast, down south to the Mexican border and all the way back towards the South East he entered the Southern States for the first time. As often, he was waiting at the Greyhound Bus Station, which was situated in a rather neglected part of the city and therefore quite filthy, and made use of the time he had to wait for the connecting bus to experience the atmosphere around there. It was not without reason that he was travelling on his own because he wanted to have as many possible authentic encounters with people who lived in the particular area. By doing so, he thought he would get the best chance to get to know the country and the people.

'Although he had experienced this situation of waiting many times during his trip, this time it was different. Most of the people waiting were Americans of African origin, so he stood out markedly being caucasian with a mountain rucksack on his back. He was happy that the other people did not take any notice of him. He had often been warned by other people that the areas around bus stations were dangerous since there were "all kinds of people" hanging around there. He had not been deterred by those warnings, but he had become more cautious since his rucksack with its whole contents had been stolen at one bus station during his journey.

'After the bus had arrived and the passengers had boarded, the usual Greyhound ritual started: the driver walks through the rows and checks the tickets, then he announces on the speaker: "This is a non-smoking . . . " As always, he had found a seat in the rear third of the bus so as not to be dazzled and woken up by the headlights of approaching cars during the night. The other passengers had begun to make themselves comfortable for the night. Afterwards it became loud on the bus, as the people who knew each other started talking to each other. He noticed that their vernacular differed from the one he had previously heard in the States: it was somehow different and louder. It was only then that he realized that he was the only white person on the bus, which had happened to him for the first time on his journey. To make sure he was right he looked back and eventually took it for sure. The other passengers did not take any notice of him, whereas he started to become aware of the unusual situation. Previously he had met several black people at different occasions on his trip, but always out of a majority position. This time he was only surrounded by Americans of African origin, which provided him vividly with the "authentic experience of the people".

'He had found a seat next to a black woman with a voluminous body, since he rather chose to sit next to a woman in this unusual situation. However, she needed more than just her own seat and also used some part of his. As he was slim there was enough room for both of them. Although he usually found it easy to get in contact with other passengers sitting next to him, he found it difficult that time. In fact, he greeted her in a friendly way, but they never got into further talking during the whole journey. However, he felt disturbed by her when she started unpacking her knitting-needles and began moving them up and down in front of his head. She did not seem to bother that he could feel disturbed by that. It even made him aggressive, but he did not want to let her know. Somehow he thought that it was the way black people did it and hence he subjected himself to that cultural behaviour. He could at least get her to narrow the radius of the movements of the needles by taking out a book and holding it demonstratively in front of his head when reading it. He thanked her for that and she answered with a nodding gesture, which he interpreted as "OK".

'When thinking about the situation he remembered his early school days when they had a collecting box carrying a black little boy with little clothing on the teacher's desk. It carried a text saying "Collections for mission in Africa". Like all the other friends at school he had always asked his parents for coins to give to the "poor little Nigger Boy". Once one put the coin in the box, the "little black Nigger Boy" would nod with its head, which had

had a very motivating effect on the children. Thinking back he found it very absurd.

'By looking closer at the black passengers on the bus the perception of the neat child on the mission box disappeared in the memory in favour of the perception of the real people who were adults of different ages. The form of their heads appeared rather clumsy and seemed almost threatening to him. He could not make out why they appeared to him that way. Perhaps it was also the smell which soon filled the inside of the bus. It reminded him of a particular kind of spice he had come across for the first time when he was invited for lunch in a suburb of Chicago by a black family on his trip, which he did not particularly like.

'He recognized that smell again and found it unpleasant in the closed area of the bus and quite penetrating in its intensity. Trying to check up on it he noticed that a couple of rows in front of him some passengers had unpacked their lunches and had started eating them. That intensified the smell on the bus even more. Still today, many years after, he can identify the former smell and associates it with negative feelings. Besides, he noticed that they were eating their sandwiches with loud noises and that they threw the wrapping paper on the floor, which he found disturbing as well. In any event, the smell and the noises spoilt his appetite so that he himself did not unpack his lunch and rather tried to get distracted by reading a book.

'It had meanwhile got dark outside, which made the atmosphere on the bus even more peculiar. He was caught by a strange feeling. He did not know if it was the fear that something could happen. He remembered the game "Who's afraid of the Black Man?" from his early childhood memories and was surprised how strongly this image had become resistant in his memory. It was probably also a feeling of strangeness, since it was the first time for him to ethnically belong to the minority. From this experience he also became conscious what it must mean for somebody to be in the minority. The more so he was happy when they had reached their destination the following morning, where he was met at the bus station by his friend. For the first time he felt belonging to somebody of his colour of the skin.'

DEVELOPING SHARED OWNERSHIP OF MEMORIES

It is important not to read these two pieces of writing as 'before' and 'after' texts and to search for evidence of reformed racism in them. In the second text the writer remembers new things, puts a different emphasis on aspects of his account but does not try to expunge his racism from memory or rephrase things in a politically correct form. What is important is what the group learns from the discussion; the text is provided as a means of provoking and disciplining the discussion, not as evidence of pre-test and post-test achievement.

This example of a memory and its reworking by the group does give an idea of the nature of the research processes within a memory-work group. Such work does not have to be seen as self-contained, and often members of the group use the experience to write about the topic in ways that draw on the discussion but make little reference to the memories themselves (Frigga Haug's most recent book has a form of this kind).

One of the aspects of memory-work that does not transpose well onto the page is the way that the memories that are contributed to and worked on by the group lose their sense of author[ity] during the process. Reading this account it might seem that the person who wrote this memory would feel closely scrutinised by the other group members, in a way reminiscent of psychotherapy or a creative writing discussion group. This is not our experience; on the contrary, we have been surprised at the way that the memories shared within the group quite quickly become shared property, almost to the point where the identification of the author is forgotten. Indeed, one of the reasons that the group can engage in critical discussion is the fact that the person who wrote it is not made vulnerable and does not need to be protected by the other members of the group. What is under scrutiny are the shared responses of each group member in the face of those facets of the memory that transcend idiosyncrasy.

As we mentioned earlier, memory-work works best when the group is a real group, that is a group with shared values who want to share each other's company. Both the Berlin Group (Haug) and the Sydney Group (Crawford) were groups of women who met out of the desire to share ideas and interests before they turned to memory-work as a method. Some researchers have tried using memory-work in other circumstances – courses like the one we have described here and the HIV/AIDS research project developed by Susan Kippax. It seems that sometimes these groups work well, and other times they don't and that what determines success is in part the development of the group as a group. Memory-work requires both a serious intent and a degree of conviviality. It is not like a focus group or a T-group but then again it is not quite like a group of friends either, content just to enjoy one another's company in an unfocused way.

SELF AND RESEARCH

Social science has only recently come to realise that 'subjectivity', rather than threatening claims to scientific status, actually marks claims to disciplinary uniqueness. The task of social research has to involve both the exploration of the subjective nature of knowing and the mapping of the world as it is experienced by others. When we referred to the 'self as a re/source for re/search' in the title of this chapter we may have led you to believe that we would discuss some of the issues of subjectivity and research that are current in the methodological literature (Lather 1991, for instance). The fact that we have not done so is a consequence of a related theme that is predominant in this book, the complex interrelationship between the personal and the social. Collaborative memory-work, as we have described it, is concerned with a particular way of thinking about subjectivity as it is expressed in specified social contexts, involving ways of thinking about the self, and changing the self, that are socially rather than individualistically located. In this sense it indicates a reaction to the forced separation of self and society that marks much of social theory.

Adopting forms of research in which groups mobilise their own intellectual resources provides one way in which methodology can escape the traps set by individualism. Another means to similar ends is to move away from language as the sole source of data to using images and pictures. This is a theme we will pick up in Chapter 4.

MEMORY-WORK: A SUMMARY

The following notes were developed by Barbara Schratz-Hadwich from workshops with Frigga Haug.

Why memory-work?

- Women's experiences are absent from theories of socialisation.
- To understand those experiences new methods must be found.
- Our experience of everyday life is marked by domination and power. If we are to understand it, the structures lying beneath our experience must be made visible.

What are the assumptions made in memory-work?

- Memory-work enables us to ask how the process of socialisation works within our experience as individuals. The central topic of research is the connection between individual and social structures.
- Time is inscribed in personality. 'Personality' is constituted by memory and animated by self-consciousness (Who am I? Why am I?). The personality narrates to itself stories selected from its history and past. Why are these stories chosen and not others?
- The relationship we have to our past/personal history gives us a guideline to the present and the future: by re-considering the past you can act to change your present and future.

What does memory-work do?

- Memories are not seen as pictures of people's experience, but as a process of selectively choosing, arranging and presenting experiences. Memory-work interrogates this process rather than the memories themselves, asking how and why we recall, and relive, events in the way we do.
- People recall their memories and reconstruct their experience, re-arranging them so that they can live alongside them with the minimum of contradiction or inconsistency. The way that they do this determines how they act and respond to the situations in which they find themselves.
- In asking how experience is reproduced in memory, we find out where we compromised without realising it. Failing to see the alternatives that become obscured by the actions we take may be to restrict our sense of our own potentials and capabilities. Re-discovering these possibilities we regain new chances and different possibilities to act in the present and in the future.
- We also learn how we accept, incorporate and become part of existing structures and so how we become a part of society.

In what ways is the use of memory-work productive?

- Language: it provides new ways of looking at the ways in which we use language, the relation of language to memory and to socialisation. It also provides a way of looking at the uses we make of metaphors, clichés, etc.
- Confrontation with the tacit knowledge that is taken for granted in everyday life and the theories that underlie it. This can give us a way of working with those aspects of personality that we are normally aware of as prejudice, as emotion and blind preference. To make this process we must go beyond using text for purposes of self-verification and move to collaborative action. Only collaborative groups can do memory-work.
- Existing theories do not consider personal experiences, or do so inadequately. Memory-work provides a way of looking at the social world which is distinctive and different. It constitutes a theory, not just a method.

How does memory-work work?

- It is similar to a process of guided biography.
- It is a collective method:
    concerned to bring others' stories closer to our own experience,
    interested in the ideas, wishes and feelings of the author,
    searching for gaps and blind spots,
    asking for the identification of emotions.

- Texts are written in the third person since:

    faced with beginning with the first person often means that women tend to write too little about themselves,

    sticking to the text prevents the group from straying into interpretation,

    using the third person establishes that each author is both the object and the subject of research.

What are the steps to be taken in memory-work?

- After the first reading of the texts one is selected as a starting point and the first impressions of the group are taken (asking for instance: 'What does the author say her problem is?' 'Which theories does she seem to have?'). These impressions are written down so that, at the end, they can be compared to the final understanding the group has achieved (since memory-work discussions on one piece may be sustained over long periods sometimes we find that the problem has become displaced, or that the questions have changed).
- The group analyses the text. In doing so it is important not to get stuck in pursuing individual group members' own feelings or interpretations. Memory-work is different from literary criticism and not at all like therapy. Looking to get behind the text by a process of interpretation does not get you any further!

Practical rules

1 To start, try to ask questions of the text which must be answered with the words and phrases contained within the text, about the:
    - activities of the author,
    - feelings of the author,
    - interests, wishes of the author,
    - activities of the others,
    - feelings of the others,
    - interests of the others,
    - language,
    - blind spots, gaps,
    - connections and contradictions.

2 Then ask questions about the text concerning its construction. These questions require answers that cannot be taken from the text directly and concern the:
    - construction of the self,
    - construction of the others.

3 Towards the end, reformulate the problem in the form of a thesis which:
  - starts from and directly confronts the problem of the author (rather than seeing this as illustrating a theory from elsewhere),
  - collects ideas from other texts and confronts other existing theories.

4 Being there: using pictures to see the invisible

With Janine Wiedel

Illustration 6 Janine's photographs

Illustration 6 (Cont.)

Illustration 6 (Cont.)

Illustration 6 (Cont.)

Illustration 6 (Cont.)

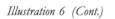

Illustration 6 (Cont.)

Illustration 6 (Cont.)

CATALOGUE NOTES

Across the social sciences there has been a curious neglect of the visual imagination. Curious because, while social science has spent much of this century trying to establish its credentials as 'science', it has tried to do so, until quite recently, by the compulsive adoption of quantitative methods and the framing out of all that might be thought of as pictorial. Social scientists almost always look on pictures with suspicion, knowing the capacity of photography to manipulate meanings, sceptical of the motivations of photographers and seeing pictures of any kind as unreliable sources of documentary evidence. Yet, meanwhile, science itself has become more and more dependent on visual information and more sophisticated in finding new forms of visual representation for that which is normally invisible and can be 'seen' only through machines – microscopes, telescopes, traces on film or complicated methods of computer enhancement. In science, only routine data are presented as numbers (the kind of research some scientists refer to, mildly derogatorily, as 'handle-turning'); almost everything at the frontiers of knowledge has to be visualised.

Paradoxically, a significant cost of the framing of social science as an empirical, objective way of studying social life has been the loss of opportunities to understand much of the complexity of social relationships and so a silence has grown in a significant area of theory. Social scientists have concentrated most of their efforts on looking at human action (from a safe distance), not looking into it (from close up), since to do so would be considered to risk objectivity. (There are of course exceptions; for a recent review of the field and an exploration of the links that can be made between visual art and social science see Chaplin 1994.) For instance, we think that the photographs that open this chapter have a good deal to say about the human aspect of life in classrooms, for they show the camera being used as what Australian cartoonist Michael Leunig might call an 'Understandascope' (Illustration 7). But despite a strong interest among sociologists and educational researchers in the research problem of how to understand classroom life, a research interest that has been energetically and enthusiastically sustained for the last twenty-five years, evidence of this kind is always left outside the frame. Instead researchers have used transcripts of what teachers and students say to one another, what they have said to the researcher ('the interview'), and what teachers might have said to themselves (in a journal). Despite an enormous research literature that argues the contrary, researchers have trusted words (especially their own) as much as they have mistrusted pictures. (See Jack Sanger's 1993 paper for some consequences of this uncritical trust in words.) But they have mostly not seen that this train of words leads directly back to similar problems of representation and

Illustration 7 Michael Leunig, 'The Understandascope'

authority. Central to the dilemma they face is the need to understand how the author/photographer mediates meanings between the evidence and the reader. Is the author concerned to impose authority? Does he or she see their task as exposition, as beginning a conversation or perhaps as a moral crusade? Whereas, for the readers, the task is to see through and past the writer, not to be told what to think but to develop their own capacity for criticism. As Roland Barthes starkly puts it in an often used quotation: 'the birth of the reader must be at the cost of the death of the author' (Barthes 1977: 148).

In this chapter we will consider two kinds of pictures, photographs and drawings. We do not intend to review the various ways such pictures have been used in research but to continue the theme of the nature of the involvement of the researcher in the process of research. The photographer, like the ethnographer, derives authority from being a trusted witness, but the photograph (especially the private photograph) draws its warrant from its relationship to memory and the reconstruction of history. Sometimes the photographer can get caught between being the observer and being a witness – look again at the expression on the face of the 'understandascope' operator. The use of pictures in research therefore raises in a different form the continuing question of the relationship between public and private knowledge and the role of research in tracing and transgressing this boundary.

BEING THERE

'Unlike photographs, literary representations do not prove that the author was there', write Judith Okely and Helen Callaway (1992: 23) in the somewhat contorted negative logic consequent on the social scientist's suspicion of the pictorial. In the photographs that open this chapter the photographer was clearly there; we can almost feel ourselves to be in her space and the eyes that look at her look also at us. (The introduction to Clifford and Marcus' book *Writing Culture* (1986) makes a similar point.) A photograph, like a film, creates an immediate if vicarious sense of being there that is stronger than most readers will get from reading an ethnographic description or selected interview transcripts. Yet the authorship of text, as Geertz (1988) demonstrates, is also concerned to mark the author's rights of possession and ownership: the reader is allowed to look but not to touch. The author points out to you the written artifacts he or she has taken from the field, much as if they were in a museum, but in these photographs it as though Janine says, not 'look at what I have found' but 'come with me, and look!' The appropriate metaphor is not that of being taken through a museum but of being guided on a field trip, or being invited to travel with her to some normally unfrequented or inaccessible place. Having looked at these pictures we will look differently at what we see in classrooms.

There are strong similarities between the work of ethnographers and that of photographers, both go into the field and return to tell us of the uniqueness of the experiences they have had. As readers we know that this is not quite the same as being there ourselves but a more important difference is that where the photographer aims to capture and preserve critical moments, the ethnographer is concerned to move from fieldnotes to a monograph, to transcend particularity in pursuit of theory. This is reflected in the distinction ethnographic researchers invariably make between 'writing down' and 'writing up' (Fabian 1988), since this implies a separation between taking and making which is at the heart of the ethnographic enterprise.

Photographs retain a sense of always being in the present. Research may mimic this by a sleight of hand that is often used in qualitative studies; the reporting of the past in the present tense, since we often give accounts of people, events and situations as we found them or as they described themselves to us. In trying to persuade the reader in a way that retains the vividness they first had for us we may continue to use the present tense, even though the research report may be published after the event. If you look and read carefully you will find us doing this here on a number of occasions in this book! What might seem at first to be an arbitrary grammatical decision has more significant consequences than you might suspect. One consequence is that it is not uncommon for those implicated in our accounts to say, 'That is how it was, but it has changed since you were here, yet you write about it as if things have not changed.' This may not trouble the social analyst whose concern is with developing theory but it has more serious consequences for the researcher who is inside the situation or who intends that their research will be closely associated with action. The conservatism inherent in ethnography appears at first sight to disqualify its use in the context of action research, for ethnography is always concerned with what was (even if it describes what 'was' in a continuous present tense). Action research, in contrast, is concerned with improvement and change, with achieving now what otherwise might remain unrealised. But we have overdrawn the distinction, ethnography is useful in the context of change precisely because it identifies what remains unchanged, it looks behind surface appearances to continuities and consistencies that might at first be hidden. Its concern is always to ask if the world is as people say it is and to explain it by connecting personal experiences and social structures.

If ethnography is to be used in this way in the kinds of situations that concern us, the researcher has to be careful not to become flooded with descriptive data and so drawn away from the critical tasks of analysis and interpretation. Ethnography is in essence a theoretical preoccupation, though in the forms in which it has been adopted by educators and other professionals it may appear as a one word justification for copious atheoretical description.

The way that tense is used both in descriptive reporting and in social analysis is somewhat more complex than a simple recourse to the ubiquitous use of the present. John Davis (1992) has pointed out that a characteristic of anthropological writing is its habit of moving between the present tense and the past, often within the ambit of a single sentence. 'Case-histories, illustrative incident, are the photographs of ethnography', he writes (and in continuing the sentence he exemplifies his own analysis), 'we have generally written about them in the past tense and discussed them in the present' (Davis 1992: 210).

In ethnographic writing, the use of the present conveys an authenticity to the writing – emphasising that the author was there and the observations he or she has made can be trusted, while the past tense tends to be used mostly for the data, for descriptions and generalisations made from descriptions. In the kind of research that concerns us here, we may choose an ethnographic style and report events in the grammatical past, or we may keep our descriptions in the present so as to keep our observations alive and fresh. We may be especially tempted to keep to the present tense when we have extensive transcripts and field notes from which we can quote. To do so leads to a sometimes effective but curious use of grammar, because while we might write in the present we do so within a frame that locates our account in the past. In this sense it is not unlike writing a script for a film or a play or writing dialogue in a novel, it is a device for bringing the reader to a certain level of involvement and expectation by a displaced use of the present tense. Like the language of children it collapses the distinctions created by a sense of time. Similar comments could be made about memories, for memories are both in the present and of the past, and in the previous chapter we showed how their frames can be opened so that they can be revisited, revised and reworked so as to have different meanings in the present.

The fact that pictures have this quality of maintaining a present tense while being displaced in time gives them a particular power when used in social research for they allow us to represent events to people as if they were still happening. Photographs have a double border, the 'frame' in the sense that photographers use the term, to mean what is contained within the viewfinder (and what is selected out), and the 'frame' created by the way we talk about the photograph, particularly in the way we locate it in time as an indicator of memories. John Berger has pointed out that photographs (at least those he calls 'private photographs', the pictures we have of ourselves, friends and family) are closely associated with memory, sometimes painfully so. For example, he and his collaborator, photographer Jean Mohr (1982), describe their attempts to record the life of an alpine farmer in Switzerland. They take (notice our use of tense here!) numerous photographs of him at work, milking the cows, cutting hay, preparing his meals, but he rejects them all as a record for his grandchildren to see and chooses instead to be photographed in a suit he rarely wears except to church, and in a pose that is unlike his 'natural self'. In this his views are not unlike those of the Chinese Government in the 1970s whom Susan Sontag quotes as rejecting Michelangelo Antonio's film about China because they see it as setting out morally to degrade the peasants by catching them unawares (Sontag 1979).

Pictures, it seems, have a power that words often lack. Taking a photograph is a process subject to all kinds of distortion but nevertheless the photograph has a verisimilitude that is undeniable (Roland Barthes (1982: 209) describes it, perhaps mistakenly, as 'a message without a code'). In social research pictures have the capacity to short circuit the insulation between action and interpretation, between practice and theory, perhaps because they provide a somewhat less sharply sensitive instrument than words and certainly because we treat them less defensively. Our use of language, because it is so close to who we are, is surrounded by layers of defence, by false signals, pre-emptive attack, counteractive responses, imitations, parodies, blinds and double blinds so that most of the time we confuse even (perhaps, especially) ourselves. In this maze of complexity pictures can have a use, to use John Collier's phrase, like that of a can opener (Collier 1967). The point is, not to use pictures instead of words, but to use them in order to create a context within which to talk and to write.

Where photographs can take us behind the scenes and allow us to share witness with the researcher, drawings can take us inside the mind of the subject. While there are dangers in taking this window on the mind too literally, the ways in which people draw things, their relative size and placement of objects for example, can at least give us a starting point from which to ask questions. In what follows we will give some examples of the creative uses of drawing in research. Unlike photography, the use of drawings has a minor but extended tradition of use in social science, but almost always drawings have been treated as an external source of non-verbal data. For instance in intelligence testing, the 'draw-a-man' test has been used to get some measure of pre-literate intelligence and the similar 'draw-a-scientist' test to reveal stereotypical images that might be more closely guarded by tact, politeness or political correctness when verbalised. Following our discussion of memory-work and the suggestion that photography might be used in parallel ways, we approach the use of drawings with a somewhat different perspective.

WATCHING TV WATCHING

Susan Groundwater-Smith was commissioned by the Australian Broadcasting Company to provide them with a study of educational television use in schools (Groundwater-Smith 1990). She had been interested in the work of Patricia Palmer, a media researcher, who had collected drawings from children of their television watching at home which had showed this to be a much less passive, and much more social, activity than media researchers and others had often supposed (Palmer 1986).

Following this lead, Groundwater-Smith asked primary school children to draw pictures of themselves watching television at home and in school (Illustration 8). The pictures they gave her of TV watching at home replicated Patricia Palmer's evidence. They would often record a face on the screen, as though the TV was someone to whom they could relate. The children would often be involved in multiple activities while the TV was switched on, eating, drinking, talking, playing with the cat or the dog; all activities that would be missed by the 'peoplemeter'. The way they represent their posture in their drawings is interesting. At home they would look comfortable, often they would not be seated in a chair, but lying on the floor with toys, games, books and other 'distractions' close at hand. Often they would be holding the remote control in their hands as they channel hopped or grazed through the medium.

Watching television in school was a quite different kind of activity.

home

i'm pippilongstocking

School

I made
this up
because I
didn't
really like
the shows
at school

Watching television at school — teacher's
choice.

Watching television at home — being in control.

Illustration 8 Watching television at home and at school

Home

School

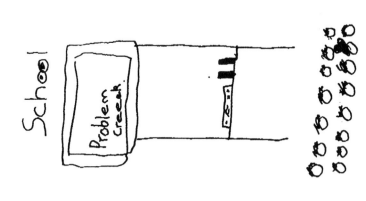

Problem creeek

Watching television at home — familiar
objects, favourite shows.

Watching television at school — one
of many before a large monitor.

Illustration 8 (Cont.)

Children sat upright, sometimes in ordered rows of chairs looking up at a screen set high above their heads, there were no distractions to hand and if anyone held the remote control it was the teacher. Often nothing would be recorded on the screen, though sometimes words would issue forth. The scene seemed almost a parody of the nineteenth-century classroom attempting 'simultaneous instruction' (Hamilton 1989).

These differences between home and school seem not to be just differences in context but differences in content and attention. The TV at home seems a much more animated device than the one at school, which seems to be seen as like the voice of a distant teacher. Susan Groundwater-Smith's conclusion that watching television at school is a quite different experience from watching it at home, is one that television programmers and producers would be unlikely to consider without this kind of evidence. While they might draw on audience research to identify a particular 'demographic', taking into account the immediate social context within which the viewer watches television has not been a consideration for most people on the production side of the screen.

CHILDREN AND DRUGS

Pictures can be used to cut through some of the levels of pretence, posing and edited self-presentation that frequently dominate our responses when, as subjects, we are faced with completing a questionnaire, being asked questions in an interview or being part of a discussion in a focus group. Pictures can be useful too when we don't want the question we ask to pre-determine the answer we will get, either by virtue of its content or its tone. (Tom Logan (1984) gives some good examples of the way interviewees hide their responses from interviewers according to the way that they perceive the interviewer as a person.)

In the next study we will describe, Ann Collins investigated the understandings that primary school children have of 'drugs'. The study was a replication of a study devised in England by a group at the University of Southampton who produced a booklet called *Jugs and Herrings* (the title refers to the misperceptions, or perhaps reconstructions, of the words 'drugs' and 'heroin' by children in the study). In her study, Collins asked children at lower-, middle- and upper-grade levels in three schools in Geelong, Victoria, to respond to the following questions:

First question
 Ann: Linda was walking home when she found a bag with drugs inside it.
   Draw what you think was in the bag.
   Write at the side of it what it is you have drawn.

(For each question, Infants were asked – Tell me what you have drawn and I will write it for you.)

Second question

Ann: Who do you think lost the bag? Draw the person.
Write at the side the type of person you have drawn.
Third question

Ann: Draw what you think that person was going to do with the drugs.
Write your answer.

After they had done this, the children were asked two further questions:

Fourth question

Ann: Draw what you think Linda did with the bag.
Write what she did.

Fifth question

Ann: What would you have done if you had found the bag?

Illustration 9 shows some of the responses from the children.

Ann Collins had a number of reasons for carrying out this study in the way she did and presenting it in this form. First, she was able to suggest some statements about the data which might be generalisable. For instance, in her summary she wrote:

Participants in this research recognised both legal and illegal drugs. Cigarettes, in particular, were frequently nominated as the 'drugs in the bag'. But it is interesting that even when the bag contained legal drugs the response was to 'take them to the police' or, in infant grades, 'throw the bag away'.

The common perception of a drug user was of a male teenager. The wide variety of responses indicated though that many were aware that people of different ages and in various situations take drugs. There were associations between drug use and the person who was sad, without a home or had problems. Overall, males were connected more with the world of drugs than females.

(Collins 1991: 15)

Second, she could make some comparisons with the English study, in which they used their data to identify the ages at which children had particular levels of understanding and to see at what ages they seemed to be most influenced by different sources of information (parents, the media and peers). Like the first study she found a big jump in sophistication in middle grades and signs of influence from the media.

Third, she wanted to find ways of asking the questions which allowed the children to respond in ways that seemed 'natural' and did not put them

PREPS

Drawings labeled: PUT THEM IN THE BIN; A GIRL; DRUGS; THROW THEM IN THE BIN BECAUSE THEY WERE BAD LOLLIES; A GIRL WITH CURLY HAIR AND A SPOTTY DRESS; LOLLIES CHOCOLATE MILKSHAKE; TAKE A DRUG; A GIRL; CIGARETTES

Illustration 9 'Jugs and herrings'
Source: Collins 1991

Drugs was the most common response. One child thought bugs were in the bag. Answers ranged from smokes, needles and pills to crayons, a rabbit, poison and Pepsi.

Either a boy, man or girl lost the bag. Someone thought a father lost it, another that it was a lady.

The person was going to throw the drugs away, or use them (drink, puff, smoke or eat). The child suggesting bugs were in the bag thought the person would get a mozzie catcher.

5 year olds

Lollies, Smarties, Prima, chocolate or a milkshake were in the bag. Smokes, alcohol and tablets were also mentioned. One child thought the bag contained what mummies drink.

A girl lost the bag. Others thought a rock 'n' roll man, a teenager, an old person, a mother.

The drugs were going to be used (drunk, eaten, smoked), taken home, or thrown away. One child thought the person was going to kill somebody with the drugs.

Illustration 9 (Cont.)

NEELDES, SMOKES, MATCHES

PILLS, SYRINGE, COCAINE, HEROIN

CIGARETTES, SYRINGE, PILLS, MEDICINE, BEER

GRADE SIX

PUNK

SMOKING

A DRUG ADDICTED JUNKIE

SHALLOW THE PILLS, PUT THE SYRINGE IN HER AND SELL THE COCAINE AND HEROIN

PUNK DRUG ADDICT

SELL THEM TO OTHER PEOPLE

Grade six

Smokes, needles or marijuana were in the bag. Other responses included a range of legal (beer, tablets) and illegal (heroin, speed, cocaine) drugs.

A street kid, a punk, a drug addict or a drug dealer lost the bag. Other responses included a drugo, a drunk, a bum, a criminal, someone needing money, a teenager and someone with bloodshot eyes and lots of problems.

The person was going to sell them. Others thought they would be used – smoked, injected, drunk, sniffed.

Syringes and needles were the most common responses. Others thought drugs, tablets, pills, heroin, powder, cocaine or marijuana were in the bag.

Any number of people might have lost the bag – a junkie, a business man, an alcoholic, a smoker, a street person, a stressed man, a runner, a punk, a psycho man, a girl with problems, someone sad, angry or weary.

The person was either going to take the drugs or sell them.

The bag contained cigarettes, pills, medicine, beer, steroids, cocaine, syringes, crack, marijuana or heroin.

A punk, a boge or a drug addict lost the bag. Other responses included a drunkie, a smoker, a business man, a bad person wanting to make money and a person who needs help.

The drugs were gonig to be sold.

Illustration 9 (Cont.)

Illustration 9 (Cont.)

under undue pressure. By making the activity 'fun' she was not risking associating the topic of drugs with undue moral seriousness. If she had entered the school in a white coat and extracted children from their classes to quiz them about drug use she would have been in danger of acting with an undue measure of methodological violence. But it is interesting that although university ethics procedures required 'informed consent' to a 'plain language' summary of the study, obtaining such consent is not necessarily as neutral an activity as it is made to sound. The meaning and purposes of research (and the role of the researcher) carry heavy cultural connotations for most people. When we ask questions of people in the context of research, often these questions are seen to be imbued with authority. While our failure to be explicit about our research to our subjects can be seen to be taking undue risks with the lives of others, the process of seeking consent too can be interventive.

Fourth, Collins used this approach deliberately to mimic advertising methods. The issue of advertising legal drugs is a contentious one, but the response of drug research to criticism has often been one of flight to figures. When put under the pressure of public scrutiny, researchers tend to retreat to what they consider safe ground, in this case leaving the field of images open to advertisers to exploit. In this sense, this (admittedly very small) study was intentionally political, a small attempt to reclaim the territory abandoned by drug researchers.

These examples show some of the ways in which visual methods can be used. The 'draw-a-scientist test', which is perhaps better known than the examples we have given here, almost always reveals the images children accumulate from the media of eccentric asocial men in white coats and beards whose life is dominated by the pursuit of Armageddon-like inventions (usually in test tubes and somehow involving high electric voltages) and over which they have almost no control.

PERCEPTUAL MAPS

Somewhat more abstract is the use of diagrams rather than representative drawings. Lindsay Fitzclarence has used this technique as part of a set of exploratory interviews he conducted with groups of senior secondary students about the way they see their time at school as part of their lives (Fitzclarence 1991a). In the course of the interview he gave each student a sheet of A4 paper and said to them that if this paper represented their lives, how did the various aspects of their lives relate to one another?

> I met the (year 11) students at Alice's home one night after school and the discussion was taped. In the discussion we concentrated on what was involved in a typical week and the dominant theme was that of dealing

with an intense and complex set of demands. I asked them to draw where time was spent and then followed this with a second drawing which showed 'How I would like to spend my time'.

Alice commented on her first drawing 'When I am home I am always at my desk. I hardly see any of my family. . . . It's just like being at school, but you're in a different room.' When we explored the places she would like to spend time, 'more time outside' and 'socialising with friends' were the main choices.

. . . I think this issue of control over time is emerging as a major theme. The amount of time spent in 'busy work' and the need to adopt a

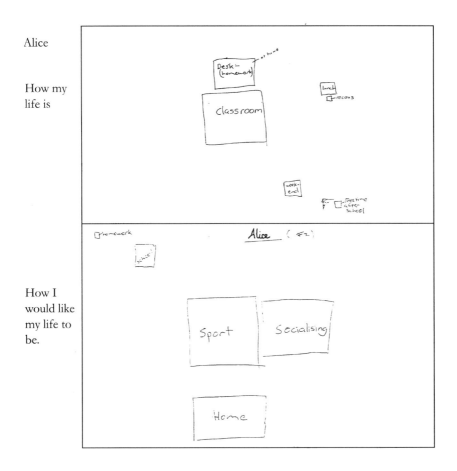

Illustration 10 Alice's 'mattering maps'

study habit have become part of the persona, but experienced as something 'alien'.

(Adapted from Fitzclarence 1991a)

Illustration 10 shows the mattering maps which Alice drew. You can see that, unlike the standard questionnaire item, the response gives more information than is contained by the question. It is not just that the relative size of the areas can be informative. The way they relate to one another, the sequence in which they are given, the shapes given to each activity and its location on the page all provide prompts that can be followed up in the interview. Perhaps more important, starting an interview like this, and using the response as an agenda for the interview, gives the person some degree of involvement and even some control over the topics to be discussed. The effect on the interview itself can be important, for instead of the interviewer holding all the cards (sometimes literally) and quizzing the interviewee, who has no clues as to what she will be asked next, here both interviewer and interviewee can address the diagram, adding a third point of reference and so taking the pressure off the interviewee to perform.

DIFFICULTIES WITH MATHEMATICS

The pictures that the children drew of themselves watching TV are not the same as photographs we might have taken of them at the time. The drawings draw on subjective elements of the experience, perhaps magnifying them in the process. The projective quality of drawings is one of their most interesting features, but it may be difficult to get adults to draw, because drawing is one of those skills that most adults feel reveals their lack of competence. For most children, drawing is a natural form of expression, but adults are often hard to persuade that drawing is a form of expression rather than a test of competence. But adults will feel comfortable looking at photographs and may be persuaded to comment on what they see. Moira Bovill (1990) used this natural communicative power of photographs to investigate the experiences of adults who had had great difficulties with mathematics during their formal education. Faced with collecting research data to inform television producers who were planning a series of programmes in basic adult education from people who might be reluctant to talk, Bovill asked a sample of adults who had experienced difficulties with maths to choose photographs which represented their feelings about learning maths at school and asked them to explain why they had chosen these pictures.

Two examples make the point. One picture that was chosen was of a station attendant at a Tokyo railway station packing commuters into a train so that the doors might be closed. Two people who chose this photograph commented:

> *Susie:* I couldn't cram it all in at all. It was just hopeless. There was just too much trying to get in and hardly any of it could. I didn't really understand it.
>
> [Aged 35]

> *Ann:* I felt the teachers kept pushing you and pushing you, and nothing sank in. Everybody else seemed to grasp it, but I never could.
>
> [Aged 39]
> (Bovill 1990: 16)

It seems that the pictures, used in this way, cut through many of the reservations people might have had about talking about a strong sense of failure in their lives. Since the topic of failure came to dominate much of the research, Bovill later asked people to identify 'successful' people from photographs.

One picture chosen was that of a smartly dressed man in a business suit talking on the telephone. The comment was:

> He's an office worker and he doesn't like anyone to get any higher up than he does.
>
> [Women's group]
> (Bovill 1990: 54)

Faced with people who may have felt threatened by direct questions, the researchers, by their use of photographs, found a way of giving people the space to express themselves in their own voices.

COUNTING THE DECKCHAIRS AS THE SHIP GOES DOWN

We have looked at two kinds of pictures, drawings and photographs, in this chapter and you might feel that to juxtapose two such different kinds of information is confusing. Our reason for doing so is that both drawings and photographs share the characteristic that they capture and retain aspects of the people they concern. The drawings the children made of drugs tell us something about those children, we may not always know what they tell us but any one child's drawing is distinctive and personal. And the photo-graphs retain the distinctive posture, expression and characteristic demeanour of the people portrayed. They are photographs of these people at this time in this place and circumstance, not of people in general. Perhaps this explains why social research has been reluctant to use pictures, for this very identification of people poses a threat to conventional notions of objectivity and raises ethical issues that research finds difficult to address.

A recurring theme in this book concerns the recognition of the person in the sight of research (to borrow a phrase from Fletcher 1975). Social research has travelled a considerable distance from the Christian views of self and society which dominated nineteenth-century thought by maintaining a tight grip on objectivity, but in consequence now finds itself in a cul-de-sac. Part of the problem we face in finding ways of research that are useable in particular contexts, at work, in the home and elsewhere, is that 'objectivity' looms as a major obstacle when our research confronts us with real people, people who can and will argue with us, question, shift the topic or deflect us from our purpose. Seeking a resolution in a technical response, whether the action research spiral, a particular therapy, clinical method or approach to organisational development, will always be at best a partial answer. What we need, is not to reject conventional objectivity, but to find ways we can move more easily between objectivity and subjectivity, between analysis and synthesis, between theoretical and intuitive, emotional and cognitive responses without losing our way. Learning to orient ourselves within such a diversity of ways of knowing is not easy, but to respond by tightening our grip on what we already know is merely to cling to the wreckage as the ship goes down.

5 Reading to write: finding songlines in the research literature

With Barbara Kamler

PEDAGOGICAL NOTES ON THE HOME FRONT

Thought: I must get my Master's dissertation proposal in to Rob tomorrow, topic: 'Decision-making by Student Teachers'. Clark and Yinger (1979) have an interesting model on pre-active and interactive decision-making.

'Mum, we're out of orange juice again.'

Thought: I wonder if Clark and Yinger (1979) ever run out of orange juice? Now if I concentrate on the educational theory versus co-operating teacher experience . . .

'Mum, it's my turn to choose the telly programme! I want to watch the A-Team!'

Thought: If you've got a problem and you can find us, we'll do our best to help (A-Team 1984). I think I'll need to observe four students in pre-instructional planning, which is related to their interactive decision-making, as did Kounin (1981), and . . .

'Mum, the big ginger tomcat's after Fluff again!'

Thought: Yes, the preliminary planning is crucial. I need to take Fluff to the vet and have a look at Shavelson's (1982) paper on judgements and decision-making. Probably I could use some stimulated recall techniques, as did Tuckwell (1979), to collect my data.

'Mum, everyone in my class has triple ear-piercing. Can I get my ears pierced on Saturday?'

Thought: The noise in a classroom can be pretty ear-piercing. I wonder what alternative decision-making is evident during overall classroom management? And Gump (1981) has some interesting research on peer pressure and student decision-making.

'Mum, don't give me salmon sandwiches again. The kids say my breath stinks.'

Thought: That article by Salmon (1983) could be useful.

'Mum, I need $4.50 for roller skating tomorrow.'

Thought: I hope she doesn't break her arm again (1983).

'Mum, he's changing the telly! The A-Team isn't finished yet!'

Thought: Yes the pace of changing decisions in favour of alternatives could be a significant factor. Perhaps I could interview the two co-operating teachers and . . .

'Mum, I can't find the Vegemite!'

Thought: Vegemite (1984).

'Mum, you shrank my Boy George T-shirt in the wash!'

Thought: If I look at the influence of educational theory (Boy George 1984) against co-operating teacher influence (Battle of Hastings 1066) I think I'll have problems. Perhaps I'd better go back to Clark and Yinger (1979) and find out if they ran out of orange juice. I'll make further decisions on decision-making tomorrow after I have rung the vet (Fluff 1984).

(Margaret F. D. Clark 1984)

Personally I haven't ever been given any sort of guidelines of how to go about it and I still don't know exactly what should be in a literature review.

Student

Although writing the 'literature review' is a standard academic task, it takes on a special significance when it forms part of the work for a thesis. In a commissioned research report the review is usually driven by content alone and with the help of a librarian it can become almost routine, but in a thesis the task takes on mythical status. Writing a research review in an academic context seems to be one of those things that is rarely taught but which we are expected to learn by some mysterious process of osmosis. We have often heard from students that they were *told* by their supervisors to *do* a review of literature, but they were never told *how* to go about it. If they consult introductory books on research methods students often find the same message – the review of the literature has to be done but they will find that there is little strategic advice available.

In some fields, supervisors may even take the view that the literature is best not taken too seriously and that consulting the work of others confuses things, as Michael Agar recalls from experience:

The next problem is to read 'the literature'. The way some social science is written, I don't know why it's called 'literature', but it is. In addition to learning something, you must also do this as part of several practical chores, like grant applications and bibliographies for graduate examinations. But there is a 'perverse streak' in some ethnographers that literature will only cloud your mind with other people's mistakes and misconceptions.

(Agar 1980: 24)

It is true that there is a vast number of textbooks which have the generic title, *Introduction to . . .*, but these seem geared to formal aspects of the actual writing of a thesis or dissertation, dealing with such things as structures, styles, references, bibliographies and similar practical concerns. There are several books available that deal specifically with techniques for writing essay reviews, for instance Pirie 1985, Cooper 1989, Schiek 1992. What remains, though, is an enormous gap between hope and happening, which opens up like an abyss confronting the student when it comes to the task. The need is for discussion of appropriate strategies. What kind of task is it? How does it relate to other aspects of the thesis? What are the common misunderstandings that can lead the unwary off track?

In a thesis, the literature review is intended to describe the 'state of play' in the area selected for study and include a critical appreciation of it. This often forms the basis for the defence of a proposal which, when successfully complete, is taken to indicate the competence of the student to proceed with field study. Since this is an area where folklore thrives and most students learn from discussing informally with one another we thought it appropriate to adopt an informal oral style, rather than an instructional style for this chapter.

What follows is a discussion between Barbara Kamler, senior lecturer in Language Education at Deakin University, and the two authors of the book. The discussion concerns the problems that arise when writing a critical review of the literature.

(The transcript has been edited; if you want to listen to the tape of the original discussion, which was first made for our research students, you will find details referenced as Kamler *et al.* 1992.)

Michael: Well Barbara, can you still think back to the time when you had to write critical reviews of literature when you were a student?

Barbara: Well, it's near history for me, it's only five years ago, I guess, and I think one of the problems that I faced was a sense of not knowing how to do it. I knew that I was doing a thesis and I was engaging in a new discourse, and I knew what the task was, but I always had the feeling of not knowing how to do it.

Michael: How did you go about it then?

Barbara: Well, I guessed a lot. I did a lot of reading of what other people had done, I tried to find some models of the way people did it. And then I spoke to people. One of the difficult things was that one of the areas was a very new one to me, and I was new at reading in the area, and I didn't know what to read, because I could have read so much, and just actually doing a literature search was not going to pinpoint what I needed to do.

So one of the things I did was go to someone who was an expert and I had quite a long conversation with her about what some of my interests were in gender and what was some of the feminist work that might be relevant. And I remember sitting in her office and her giving me lists mentioning lots of books and of course I started to read those and then go to bibliographies. That didn't actually help me write it, but it did get me into the discourse and listen to the ways she was talking about the material, which, I suppose, got me into reading what others had written, but I never had a real sense of direction. I think I kind of figured it out as I went.

Michael: What about your supervisor? Did he or she tell you how to go about it?

Barbara: Indirectly, but not directly.

Michael: I very often get the idea that people just tell you 'Go and do something about it' and you've got to find your way around.

Barbara: Do you have a memory of someone helping you more explicitly?

Michael: Not really, but what I found very helpful was with one of our supervisors; we would read a particular piece of literature and then afterwards sit together and just go through things because we found it so hard to understand the work and make use of it. So we would perhaps spend half a day and discuss just two pages. That was really helpful. What about you, Rob?

Rob: There are a number of problems that come to mind. One is the coverage versus depth problem. I think a lot of people feel they need to read everything. As an examiner I have read a lot of theses where people have read widely and reported what they have read, but failed to do what is crucial in a literature review, which is making judgements about the significance of some things as opposed to others. And I think there is a myth that writing the literature review is almost a mechanical process. If only you knew the rules, and you could pour the stuff in at one end and it would come out through the fingers that operate the word processor at the other end, so that if you gave thirty people the same task you'd end up with more or less the same literature review, and that isn't the case.

What makes the literature review work and places it in a thesis or in any other piece of work, I think, is the judgements the writer makes about what are the most important things, the ideas and the most important individual texts in the field. And I think that's what people find hard to do. The problem is getting to the point where you can make those judgements, and it's especially hard if you come from outside the field, because it's only when you have read quite a broad variety of things that you are able to do that.

For a long time, I think, the most recent thing you've read dominates everything else you've read, and you have to get to the point where that's no longer the case and it all fits a pattern.

Michael: How did you actually learn to write a critical review of the literature? Do you still remember that?

Rob: I certainly remember going through a phase of picking individual papers in journals, and from books, and then tracking down everything in the references. And everything that one person referred to I tracked back to the original sources. I guess I should have known, but it took me about a year to realise if you did that seriously, you'd end up reading everything that had ever been written, because it's all interconnected!

Barbara: I agree with what you were saying about the kind of decisions that you have to make about evaluating what the writers have said. I think it's very complex though, I think we sometimes underestimate the complex nature of the decisions about which pieces of literature you will include.

First of all, even if you are going to look at just one piece of research and summarise it, how do you decide which aspects of that study or that piece of work are relevant? You could sensibly choose a number of them, and of course, as you said, until you are more immersed in the field and have a better sense of what you're trying to achieve, you don't actually know exactly what you want to include.

So even though at one level you are involved in summarising, it's not straightforward, because you have to decide which aspect of this is going to be relevant. Am I going to look at the methodology or am I going to focus on the findings, or even on just one finding? I also feel that the review has to do with evaluation. You're not just summarising, but you are evaluating the relevance, pertinence, whatever of the work relative to your own. But probably the hardest thing is relating someone's work to all the others.

You may be reading widely, but what is the relationship between all of the things you read? I was thinking about that when you were reading everybody's bibliography because I think that's one of the ways you start to come into some kind of awareness that has to do with little clubs. Certain people cite certain people and they are all related to each other in a particular way, and I guess, that's how you extend your knowledge of the field when you're trying to figure out not only what's relevant and you're asking yourself, 'How am I going to put it together? What's valuable?' But also, what are the discourses and arguments and debates that are going on in this larger field that I've become part of, of which I only know a tiny speck? And that, I think, that's something that's hard to develop because it takes a lot of time.

Michael: I think there's so many relationships involved as you mentioned: the club, the people who are quoted there, and then the relationship, which is of course a power relationship between the text and the reader. If the reader is a student, he or she is always dependent on what the authority says, and this is what I find very hard in the critical part of the reviewing business, because what I often experience is that the students think what those people say is far better than what they think. How do you tackle that problem?

Barbara: I recently did some work with a group of students in Business, and they were writing master's degrees, and I was trying to help them write critical reviews. I knew absolutely nothing about the material that they were dealing with, and what you have just said was one of the problems that they brought up. I was trying to get them to evaluate what they had read. And one of the comments was 'How can I, the lowly student, who really doesn't know anything relative to these people and has much less experience and is much less knowledgeable, be critical of them? Am I allowed to do that? And, given my position as a student, is the examiner going to come down on me, if I make the wrong judgement?' They were very frightened to do that and it took a bit of pushing to try and get them to rewrite. They had to learn to do it because you can't just say 'I think X is idiotic', there are academic ways in which people are critical. Initially there was an enormous reluctance to do this, and I really had to spend quite a lot of time getting them to experiment and try different ways of doing it.

Michael: So you experienced that as the supervisor trying to teach those students how to go about it. Must be very hard.

Rob: It's interesting, isn't it, that a lot of people's studies will include a methodological appendix. They'll say, 'this is how I did the interviews', especially with fieldwork studies, 'this is what I did in the school and this is what happened with relationships and so on.' I can't think of anyone who's written an appendix about how they approached the literature. You have to do it, and that's part of the process you have to go through, but I don't remember reading a book or a thesis or any other published work where people have said at the end, 'here's a little section on how I actually approached the literature and how I worked through it.' There must be people who have done this, but it's not something I've come across.

Barbara: I don't think people have written about it, because I think it's part of the whole mystique of doing graduate work. If you're doing an EdD, or you're doing a PhD, you're in a domain that is more prestigious than anything you have done before. You feel you should now be intelligent and of the rank to know how to do this kind of thing. I think there is an incredible reluctance for people to ask each other or to admit, 'Listen I've read all this stuff, I don't know how to go about putting it together. I don't know what the options are. I need a place to talk to other people about some of the . . . just rudimentary ideas I have about what some of the connections are and try them out, maybe to come up with some false starts and some wrong ways of linking them, even to try out how to be critical.'

    The hard thing is how to relate one thing to another, and I think partly you have to do that by relying on your supervisor initially, and/or doing that in the way were talking about, Rob, seeing who's quoting, who's citing who . . . . That gives you some indication of what some of the connections are and what the debates are that you have arrived in the middle of. I think the trouble you have reading a text often isn't that you don't understand it, or that you're unintelligent, but that there are so many discourses and debates going on that you've come right into the middle of, that you have no idea who's arguing with who.

Rob: I've had the experience of needing to go into a field that I don't know very well (for instance in doing an evaluation study in an unfamiliar field), and you read somewhere that this particular book is a really good introduction to the field. People in the field say, this is the one that will make sense. And then you get hold of the book and open it, and it's completely meaningless and doesn't mean anything at all! It's because, I guess, you have to be on the inside to appreciate the significance of what it says and who it takes to be its audience.

Barbara: I think the whole object of doing the review is that eventually it gets you inside. Hopefully, by the time you've done it, you have an end product, but the value of this is that it's a process of getting you on the inside.

Michael: I want to come back to the point where you said that you've got to rely on what the supervisor tells you to read because you can't really read everything that's available. And that's a problem because it perpetuates the system. It means that people always read the same books.

What I have found very helpful is to rely on my students to think about what's new and what's good, rather than me telling them you should read this or you should read that, and I think that this has helped a lot in getting new perspectives. Otherwise I don't know how I could cope! I mean there's so much around. How do you cope with this?

Rob: Yes, I certainly think there's a knowledge explosion problem. There's more and more to read, and one consequence of that is either you become more and more specialised, that is you just take a very narrow field and you say I'm going to be the person who knows everything about this. Or if you try and take a wider view, you automatically face the problem that you've got to miss things out, or ignore them or take what someone else says about them as being reliable.

I think it was Einstein who said the greatest quality of the human brain is its capacity to forget, and I think you've got to have that ability to cope with an extensive literature.

But there is another fear which I know I felt and I think other people have as well, which is the fear that, just after you've written something, something much better is going to be published, which if only you'd read it, would completely change the way you've done your work.

I remember walking round bookshops looking at titles of books and my heart sinking when I saw the title of the book which was the one I wanted to write, because I thought someone's got there first . . . . And usually, when you look at it, it's completely different, it's got nothing to do with what you're on about. But I think that is the trouble with dealing with up-to-date stuff, it's the feeling that the really important text is the one that's just about to be published, which is just ahead of you in the queue.

Barbara: And then I think there comes the time when you have to stop. Sometimes you just need to rely on the supervisor to say 'Now, stop reading.' That doesn't mean that you will entirely stop, but that if you continue engaging in that process of looking, which you do get into, for the next thing and the next thing . . .

Michael: . . . you could go on for a life time.

Barbara: . . . yes, you could go on for ever. You don't want to stop too soon, but it is often very difficult to stop and most people feel guilty about stopping. I know, I do.

Rob: I'd be really interested to know how you go about recording those kind of decisions. Do you keep notes as you go? I know that some people use index cards, I guess more and more people use various kinds of computer-based systems. Do you have a recording method as you work through literature?

Michael: When I was a student I used filing cards, computers didn't exist at that time, but when I think back, it's probably only when you are a PhD student that you really take so much time in keeping track of things, certainly more than I do now. If I get hold of something now which I think is interesting or might even be interesting for some future work, I just make a copy and file it somewhere hoping that . . .

Rob: . . . you will read it . . .

Barbara: The old photocopying method, I know . . . !

Michael: . . . that's right, and you end up with all those stacks of papers . . .

Barbara: You mentioned before the difficulty of getting students to be critical. Have you found ways to help them do that?

Michael: The best way was when the students formed self-help groups to support themselves because they thought that including the supervisor was an interference. They thought, if we've got our own opinions they might not be as good as the ones of the supervisor, so we had better do it on our own. So they started writing reviews of books they'd read stating why they really liked the book and quoting passages from them. Then somebody would challenge them saying 'I see that from a different perspective.'

I think we don't make use of group arrangements enough. For some things this is better than a supervisor–student relationship that has just those two people involved.

Rob: I think there is a danger that you can fall into fashions, and we all know that academics are very good at this. Every few years will emerge the latest in-fashion author who everyone is quoting and you feel that if you haven't read them, what you are doing doesn't count for anything.

Michael: The other thing which strikes me is that we over-emphasise intellectual reading, especially as far as education is concerned. There's so much written every day in journals, in newspapers and magazines that would be valid to talk about.

Barbara: You mean journals other than academic ones?

Michael: Yes, because that's where a lot of education takes place. Otherwise we end up just talking about books which are far away from what actually happens in everyday life.

Barbara: I had a recent experience working with a student whose literature review made no sense. Not because she was unintelligent, but she had a sense that she was doing this academic act, you know – literature review . . . academic learning is baffling, it's meant to sound impressive, it's to put you on the map in some way, it's to make what you are going to look at seem relevant or of some value. With that kind of frame in her mind there was almost no logic to the kinds of categories she established in the literature review, why one thing went before the other, even what went into each category. She was writing to confound, to try and say 'Look, I am part of this field, I know how it operates' and I think, in fact, she did, but she ended up with something that was incredibly nonsensical. So she sacrificed her common sense, and everything she had known before. Entering this new discourse frightened her and made her a little bit nervous, because she felt inadequate because she had never done it before.

And that's one of the feelings that I had while I was writing my PhD, I kept feeling like I was an impostor and I kept thinking how do I know how to write this thing? Is this what it's supposed to look like, am I doing it okay? Am I impressive enough? Will you let me in? So I think that that's something worth mentioning. It's not a foreign act, but it is a new discourse act, it is new, but it's not necessary to confound, I think to me its purpose is to contextualise and to make a place for some of the things that you want to say.

Rob: I think that's exactly right, and there is that feeling that, I think, we lead people to believe through the whole education process that when you reach this point of doing a research degree, this is when the truth will be revealed.

Barbara: That's right. People will finally find you out!

Rob: I meant more that the belief that at the centre of this discipline there's something, a real truth that makes sense, and this is the point when you're going to find it. And to reach that point and realise there's only chaos, that truth is something you've got to find for yourself. That it's not something that's hidden away in say chapter seven of a book somewhere. This is a difficult thing for people to come to terms with.

I think there is a temperamental difference; some people can cope with it more easily than others. Some people do, I think, feel very threatened by the realisation that you've got to create that coherence for yourself, you're not going find it just by a mechanical reading of other texts.

Michael: And you brought in one important point I think which is worth mentioning. Who is the audience for what you write? Even in writing the critical review of literature, are you writing it as a kind of mechanical thing as you said before, as a piece before you do your masterpiece, or is it really something you want to do for somebody else and tell the supervisor or fellow students or whomever?

I think this is one of the traps in academia, that you write for ritual reasons, just to become a member of the tribe so to speak.

Barbara: But the problem is that this particular kind of text will have an examiner in the end. Anything that we can do to help people write for each other, I think, is really important, but the other reality is that at the end somebody is going to read it and judge it, and I think that is a pressure. As supervisors, we have to make sure that it's going to work with the examiners, that's our responsibility, I think.

Michael: There are so many rituals involved as you said before. I can remember very many instances in my life, especially in school, where I wasn't allowed to write what I wanted to write but what the teacher wanted to read, and that's where the problem started off, it becomes a kind of hidden curriculum to write for a non-existing audience, just for getting on.

Barbara: My experience of working with those students I was talking about in Business was that they were enormously helpful to each other. Even when they weren't necessarily reading in the same area they asked very good questions. Why did this guy say that and who disagrees with him? They asked very useful and helpful questions and they did establish a community amongst themselves. So they became much more critical readers and writers together, which they found really useful.

Michael: . . . and this makes space to experiment, especially in writing.

Barbara: People have to become confident to be able to do that, so that they won't be fearful that people will judge them.

COMMENT

In our conversation we developed the idea that the writing of a literature review, especially when this is done in the context of a thesis, is not a question of mechanically following established and agreed procedures but concerns determining significance and mapping the relationship of your work to the work of others.

For the student, the task is often felt to be a test of competence, a provisional driver's licence that gives you permission to drive around within your chosen field. But once you start moving independently within the field the problems of managing the mechanics become less pressing than the problems of route finding, reading the intentions of others and coping with logistics and time schedules.

What is important to the reader of a review is that the way that the writer refers to the literature lays down a set of markers. Knowing the signs that are indicated helps the reader develop a perspective on the study, allowing it to be located relative to ideas that are current (and sometimes less current, neglected or excluded) within the field. This is again not a simple task but involves the management of a complex semiotics. The way the writer refers to landmarks in the field indicates their relative closeness/distance to and from the work of others; even small adjustments to what is placed in the foreground and what is moved to the background may indicate a subtle placement of oneself in the academic landscape.

The scenery provided by the literature is not static; just as a landscape changes constantly as patches of cloud and sunlight move across it, sudden storms, overnight snow, the movement of the sun, the changing seasons, all change the way we see it, sometimes revealing some features and at other times obscuring them. More important still the landscape changes according to the location of the observer and the movements that they track through it and, of course, it is more like a cityscape than a natural landscape because it is constantly being added to and reconstructed.

This might explain the endless fascination with which academics observe their field, constantly reassessing it as it shifts and changes in front of them, reading the reviews, just as in everyday life we scan the newspapers and follow the weather forecasts, to give us a feeling of keeping informed and in touch with the world. Australian Aboriginal people are said to see themselves as 'belonging to' the land, and in something like this sense, academics belong to their field. Locating themselves in respect to its key ideas is not like finding their way through a library catalogue so much as establishing an identity through a songline. The alignments that biography creates, the totems and taboos, are social more than they are functional. To 'review the literature' is a statement of who you are and how you relate to others who share your culture and so, like all else in research, it turns out to be less about methods and techniques and more about identity and relationships.

6 Theory is not just theoretical

Emotion and thinking are almost inseparable. They are just different levels of the same thing.

(David Bohm 1985: 46)

In this chapter we will talk about the ways in which theory might be used in the context of the kinds of research with which this book is concerned. This is not as straightforward a topic as it might at first seem because it involves finding ways of using theory that relate to action and change, to the close interrelation of the personal and the social and to adopting forms of communication that take discussion beyond the relatively closed world of academic debate. We will, however, continue to place the discussion in particular contexts, so that what you will find in the discussion that follows is that it is about theory, and the roles that theory plays in social research, but in itself no more (and no less) theoretical than other chapters in this book.

THEORY AND RESEARCH IN EVERYDAY LIFE

In everyday conversation and in commonsense thought, most people have a clear understanding of what 'practice', 'practical experience' or 'practical knowledge' mean to them because they can instantly locate relevant references to identifiable events in their lives. This is virtually tautologous, for to say of an idea that it is 'practical' implies that it has relevance, utility and currency. Practical knowledge is what we use to make sense of our actions and those of others within the ambit of our personal and professional lives.

We tend to think of 'theory' as a different form of knowledge, more abstract and somewhat distant from everyday practicalities, yet behind what we think of as 'practical' lie theories which support this practical knowledge. We may not always make such theories explicit, still less formulate them as expository statements and propositions but, to the degree that we have the capacity to act in different ways in the face of similar circumstances, so we hold, albeit tacitly, a complex web of theories, including explanations, predictions and generalisations. Some of this knowledge we hold in the form of professional knowledge, some as craft knowledge, some as anecdote, image and expectation.

A view often expounded in social science textbooks is that the purpose of research is to replace such tacit theories with more rigorous and scientifically tested theories which are inherently of a more rational character. Empirical testing and critical analysis are presented as the processes which offer quality assurance in the development of rational theory. So, we are often given a picture of theory arising from the need to explain and interconnect demonstrated social facts in order to replace people's current theories-in-use.

In conventional theory the central move is from particular observations to generalised statements. The kind of research we advocate starts from a somewhat different premise. We see the research task, not as that of generating and sustaining generalisation, but preventing it. We believe that human thinking too readily generalises and that a key function for research is to slow down or even block this process. The research we have described in this book is aimed at making us look twice at things we observe, listen carefully to what people say and re-read texts slowly. This could be seen as advocacy for what is sometimes (disparagingly) called naive empiricism, but we are not assuming that the social world exists apart from theory and that theoretical work is the concern only of academic theorists. Our aim is to resist generalising, to scrutinise every statement for values, to search for blind spots in our own perceptions in order to understand both the espoused theories and theories-in-use of all those involved or implicated in a particular setting, event or process. We see theory as implicit in every social action, not simply the concern of academic theorists, and rather than seeking to replace these everyday theories with those we consider better, we seek to explicate and understand them. Since we believe that such theories are implicit in language it follows that we see the central methodological task being a concern with reflexivity, for language, paradoxically, is all we have to understand the social theories implicit in language.

In the normal course of our lives we learn to handle complex tasks in everyday settings, often unaware of their inherent complexity. Donald Norman, who has for many years researched the psychology of everyday things, comments on an encounter with an Austrian bus driver:

> Once, when I was at a conference at Gmunden, Austria, a group of us went off to see the sights. I sat directly behind the driver of the brand new, sleek, high-technology German tour bus. I gazed in wonder at the hundreds of controls scattered all over the front of the bus.

'How can you ever learn all those controls?' I asked the driver (with the aid of a German-speaking colleague). The driver was clearly puzzled by the question.

'What do you mean?' he replied. 'Each control is just where it ought to be. There is no difficulty.'

(Norman 1988: 25)

It is not necessary for the driver to know about the complex systems behind the controls, for their location and mode of operation has an intelligible relationship to their use and function ('Each control is just where it ought to be. There is no difficulty'). He probably got his practical knowledge about the complex control system not from lengthy lectures in his driving class, but by progressing from driving a car with a simple control panel to gaining experience driving a lorry and eventually a bus, where a great number of passengers' lives rely on his practical knowledge.

It is only when things go wrong or when we make mistakes that we have to rethink these things. In another of Donald Norman's examples of industrial design-in-use he uses photographs of glass doors in various public areas (banks, hotels, etc.) where he points out that some designs for door handles incorporate the necessary practical theory to make the act of passing through the door tacit. Only when the design is poor do we push when we should pull (though 'PULL' may be inscribed in large print on the door), or go to press the hinge rather than the handle side of the door. We have all experienced such breakdowns in design and perhaps puzzled at the way our responses to them are repeatedly replicated by others. A museum of accidents, such as Paul Virilio (1993) advocates as necessary to understand technology, would necessarily be built on the theme of breakdowns in the normal working of practical knowledge.

What would a museum of educational accidents look like?

One of the ideas we have explored in a course for experienced teachers (Deakin University 1994) is that faced with a crisis in professional practice, most people find their way out of it through a learning sequence that Chris Saville suggested to us can be described in terms of moves between stages:

From unconscious incompetence
to   conscious incompetence,
to   conscious competence,
to   unconscious competence.

The basic assumption here is that we act as though we know what we are doing until something goes wrong. When it goes wrong we experience confusion until we find some way of resolving the problem, and having done so we quickly revert to taking it for granted until it goes wrong again. This would seem to describe the situation Donald Norman's bus driver must face each time he drives a new vehicle, even if he only has to look in the manual to find out how to operate some function that is not immediately clear to him. (Though anyone who has watched children with computers will know that the manual is, for most skilled operators, a last resort.)

Making ourselves aware of what is tacit is a critical feature of the model. If we asked the question Donald Norman asked the Austrian bus driver of a professional in education or in social work, we would probably get a different answer to that which the bus driver gave. Human interactions do not usually function in the same way as a machine, even a complicated one. In dealing with human interactions simple acts have the power to represent complex values and multiple meanings. There are many meanings we carry from one situation to another, so creating large areas of ambiguity and making every interaction to some degree non-standard and non-replicable.

Jacob Kounin provides a good example of this in his book on classroom management (Kounin 1970). After numerous research attempts to identify the behaviours that make some teachers better managers of classrooms than others he encountered a case that puzzled him. In one class a teacher would signal to the students that she wanted attention by flicking the light switch off and on. Instantly the class would stop what they were doing and turn to her. But when a student teacher took over the class and tried the same move, she was completely ignored. What had the effect was not the stimulus alone, but the stimulus used in a context of shared meaning and understanding.

Even simple human interaction is generally of such complexity that we keep encountering behaviours that are unexpected and puzzling and often we are shocked to discover that a person we think we know well, even someone in our close family, has a quite different view of events which we never realise until they act in a way that is unexpected or which we are at a loss to explain. As the Elephant exercise (described in Chapter 2) demonstrates, once we have particular interpretations and ideas in mind, we tend to go to almost any lengths to avoid changing them.

THE NEED FOR PRACTICAL THEORY

One of the reasons why we need theory is to help get some grip on complexity, to narrow the problem, to develop parallels with other situations that might seem different but provide the basis for new ways of looking at things. Only theory can give us access to unexpected questions and ways of changing situations from within.

This, of course, is not to deny that there have been times in education (as in other aspects of life) when educators and others have tried to argue, and act as if, a classroom or a school worked with the precision and predictability of an electrical circuit – and they have developed theories which apparently make this possible. But human interactions do not work with the predictability we sometimes like to assume (remember the Elephant story). On the contrary, actions and operations in social settings usually become mysterious if only slight shifts are made in the context or perception of purpose that we each bring to them.

Most conventional theories operate on the assumption that explanation and prediction require us to consider only two or three variables at a time while all else can be assumed to remain constant. In any form of professional work where we are required to make frequent and rapid judgements about people in the context of intense human interaction, and where these judgements themselves quickly become part of the problem rather than apart from it, the situation itself can overwhelm the task.

A trainee teacher observes:

> Teaching which causes me to think of so many things at a time, sometimes makes me sick. I'm somehow worried about this constant pressure of having to plan. I somehow get the feeling as if I constantly had to give myself up in order to deal with all aspects.

Nor is this perceived complexity just a feature of life as a trainee. In most social situations, change, even apparently trivial change, can tilt our perspectives making us scramble to renew a sense of balance. A new child in the class; a newborn baby in the house; a new sales director in the office; a new relationship with a partner – all can transform the way we see things and the way we experience our lives. Indeed part of the appeal of such change is the challenge it presents to all that we take for granted. Changing practice always means changing one's 'practical theory' and almost always means rethinking the relationships we have with all those who are involved.

Often we talk as though 'theory' were some kind of optional academic extra – a little used switch on the researcher's dashboard to be used, perhaps, only when driving on to the campus. Here we are suggesting quite the opposite – that theory is implicit in all human action. For the teacher (as for other social professions), practical theory

> is subjectively *the* strongest determining factor in her educational practice. Counselling with teachers must consequently originate in each teacher's practical theory, seeking to foster its conscious articulation and aiming to elaborate it and make it susceptible to change.
>
> (Handal and Lauvås 1987: 9)

Yet, curiously, in conventional teacher training (as in medicine, social work and nursing), it is rarely the case that the practical theories of participating teachers are deliberately and consciously articulated. More often we ignore or suppress our own practical theories, so that they emerge only when we lose control. The reason for this is at least threefold:

1 In many situations, the options for action are limited. Often we want to change things but cannot see a way to do so. We see ourselves as limited, less by our capacity to theorise, than by organisation, resource or other considerations. Change becomes something others inflict upon us, or we expect of them.

2 Perhaps paradoxically, planned change requires a high degree of stability. The high interactive demands of teaching (as of any social work) require a high degree of predictability if the job is to be possible. Teachers who have been socialised through their own schooling as pupils and through their training as students in higher education, and who have thus acquired a working educational philosophy, cannot turn their teaching style upside down from one day to the next. Even if your practical theory of teaching is challenged in a way that causes you to question your practice, actually changing your practice is rarely easy to do and takes a long time, much longer than intellectual recognition of the problem. (That 'teachers teach as they were taught, not as they were trained to teach' is a necessary basic assumption of teacher education.)

3 Traditional pre- or in-service training only rarely provides a learning culture which promotes reflective practice. Mostly what we learn is that it is others who are experts, that errors constitute failure and that failure is not only bad but indicates inadequacy.

Educational practice is not simply less effective than it might be because we have not done enough research. A lot of research has been done, but the outcome of this research, in the form of published results and theoretical deliberations, seems to have been limited in its effects and ineffective in realising its own consequences. Little has actually changed at the 'chalk face', perhaps in part because of those same theories. Paradoxically, the idea that we can 'transfer' didactic knowledge (cf. Freire 1972), so that accumulated expert knowledge is passed on to non-experts, doesn't even seem to be used very much by educators themselves. Hartmut v. Hentig, a well-known German educational researcher and founder of the Laboratory School in Bielefeld, reports from his experiences as a university teacher:

> None of the learning objectives, hierarchical structures, goal dimensions, the operationalisation, the interesting, differentiated and plausible taxonomies, the models of input/output, stimulus/response and sender/receiver, game theory, decision-making processes and cybernetic models, systems of action and symbolic interaction, the differentiation

between teacher proof, situative and open curricula were really necessary for practical work in teaching and its planning.

(Hentig 1985: 134, translation ours)

What is the use of theories about teaching and learning if they are not 'really necessary for practical work'? Are they just abstract products made by educational researchers as they sit in their offices and laboratories and intended only for use in conferences and to further their reputations and careers as academic researchers? There seem to be two key ideas we need to consider more closely if we are to move beyond the notion of theory as just an academic game. One is the apparently abstract nature of much social theory and the other, the conventional notion of 'objectivity', and its importance to science.

ABSTRACTION

Abstraction seems to be one of the main stumbling blocks in relating theory and practice. Bruno Latour has made close observational studies of the work of scientists in the laboratory, and has tried to relate this to the 'science' that is found in the scientific literature. He tries to answer the question how it is that the 'abstract' forms of theory apply to the 'empirical world', referring here to mathematics:

'Abstract' mathematics never applies to the 'empirical world'. What happens is much more clever, much less mystical and much more interesting. At a certain point in the cascade, instruments start to inscribe forms on, for example, graph paper. A cloud of points obtained from the census through many transformations ends up, after a few more statistical rearrangements, as a line on a graph. Interestingly enough, amino acid analysers also display their results on a graph paper. More curiously, Galileo's study of a falling body also takes the form of a graph (when it is repeated today) and had the shape of a triangle in his own notebooks. Mathematics might be far from households, amino acids, and wooden spheres rolling over an inclined plane. Yes, but once households, amino acids and inclined planes have been, through the logistics above, brought onto a white piece of paper and asked to write themselves down in forms and figures, then their mathematics is very, very close; it is literally as close as one piece of paper is from another in a book. The adequation of mathematics with the empirical world is a deep mystery. The superimposition of one mathematical form on paper and of another mathematical form drawn on the printout of an instrument is not a deep mystery, but is quite an achievement all the same.

(Latour 1987: 243–4)

Bruno Latour's point is important in the present context because he sees clearly that the world of mathematics is essentially a constructed world, and a socially constructed world at that. The arguments and theories that make up mathematics might appear to be purely symbolic at first glance but they take on meaning only in an identifiable and particular social context. The very term 'argument' presupposes a particular set of social relationships which mathematics needs in order to exist. Taking this a step further, Jean Lave, at Berkeley, has explored the differences between the mathematics of experts, novices and those she calls 'just plain folks' (jpfs). Her studies of problem solving in the everyday situations in which the problems occur (the purchasing decisions made by supermarket shoppers and the maths involved in tailoring clothes, for example) lead her too to see academic mathematics as a socially constructed enterprise. We might choose to think of maths as abstract and essentially true, but it is also deeply cultural. Jean Lave writes:

> I suspect that 'knowledge domain' is in fact a name for a conventionally acknowledged claim by a social group (e.g. a profession or academic discipline) heavily invested in maintaining *its* boundaries. Control of a body of knowledge plays a major strategic role in such enterprises. If this view is correct, a 'knowledge domain' is a socially constructed *exoticum*, that is, it lies at the intersection of the myth of decontextualized under-standing and professional/academic specialization. . . . Its central char-acteristics [= of research] include the separation of form and content implied in the practice of investigating isomorphic problem solving, and a strictly cognitive explanation for continuity in activity across situations. All of these *dissociate* cognition from its contexts, and help to account for the absence of theorizing about experiments as social situations and cognition as socially situated activity. The enterprise also rests on the assumption of cultural uniformity which is entailed in the concept of knowledge domains. 'Knowledge' consists of coherent islands whose boundaries and internal structure exist, putatively, independently of individuals. So conceived, culture is uniform with respect to indivi-duals, except that they may have more or less of it.
>
> (Lave 1988: 42–3)

But seen from the perspective of the school curriculum, it is perhaps not surprising that academic theories come and go without leaving much impact on the work of practitioners or everyday life more generally, because to reach the formal abstraction required of a mathematical for-mula, requires, in almost all cases, an act of methodological violence on those situations in which we seek to improve the effectiveness of our actions. For example, despite an endless number of theories about teaching and learning existing in books and journal articles published around the world, the classroom discourse to be found in most schools is characterised by a readily recognisable pattern of teachers initiating activities, students responding to teachers' initiations and teachers evaluating students' responses. The ubiquity of this pattern has led researchers to describe classroom lessons as an unfolding series of recitation, or more recently, initiation–reply–evaluation (I–R–E) sequences (Cazden 1988, Edwards and Mercer 1987, Mehan 1979, Sinclair and Coulthard 1975). Since Socrates (at least) this pattern has persisted even though many educators have argued the need for alternative discourse in teaching and learning (Schratz and Mehan 1993).

It is easy to decry the conservatism inherent in schools and classrooms as elsewhere in society but we should not too easily neglect the fact that the resistance of social life to academic theory has important positive consequences too. Many commentators see contemporary life as too readily responding to the latest theory without scrutinising it, testing it in controlled circumstances and carefully introducing it into the mainstream of society. Indeed a chief task of many social scientists in the decades since World War II has concerned the need to build up societal protection to popular theory, particularly where it is racist or discriminatory, in much the same way as public health programmes have tried to build up immunity to epidemics.

Discussions of this issue often pose an opposition between 'theory' on the one hand and 'practice' on the other, but more properly what we encounter is a conflict between two different forms of theory. One kind of theory takes its authority from the academy and seeks to introduce radical change in the way we act in a particular setting. The other kind of theory, implicit in everyday life, tells us that deliberate change is likely to be counter-productive, since complexity makes prediction impossible. To change the world we need to understand it, but we can only understand it when we seek to change it. Devising more and more elaborate theories to account for the way the world is can have the effect of paralysing our capacity to change it. Changing things too rashly can lead us to theories which seek to explain everything and justify anything.

TAKING NONSENSE SERIOUSLY

The social world of the abstract knowledge domain identified by Jean Lave seems to be a key part of the problem in relating theory and practice as we encounter it in everyday situations. A story may help make this clear. In order to find out about the workings of an established knowledge domain and the interrelationship between understanding and professional specialisation, Wolfgang Meyer tried to use Theodor Adorno's essay 'Education after Auschwitz' in a course in a German secondary school (Meyer 1981).

Meyer was deeply struck that the students appeared untouched by the text. They consumed it indiscriminately just as they would any other teaching input, receiving knowledge about the misery of Fascism in the same way as they would read about the structure of the modern novel or the anatomy of a cow's eye. In order to press this insight further, he drafted a meaningless text consisting of commonplace statements and nonsense phrases, which were arranged in a pseudo-scientific form, and to which he gave the title 'The Dispensoric Theory of Education'.

The Dispensoric Theory of Education

What sets the thinking human being apart from others is his or her ability to think critically. Cultures appear and disappear. This is an eternal law of all biological life. A structural dialectic between innovation and stagnation can be perceived universally, a fact pointed out by the early Greek philosophers, and Euklyptos in particular. This is even true for the climate and the sequence of the seasons. Thus human society resembles a garden in which the most magnificent plants grow next to ugly weeds. If a worker wants to acquire a refrigerator in England he or she has to work for ten hours, in Argentina about ten times that long. In contrast there is hardly one village left in Africa where one would not find a radio set.

Education in Africa is different from education in America or Europe. The validity of a mathematical formula is not limited by continents. The object of the natural sciences is nature. If everything is science, everything is at the same time the subject of science. Thus, fields, woods, radio sets and human beings form a unity in the entity. In boxing it is important to knock out the opponent. The stronger wins against the weaker. Beauty as a category of nature does not play a role in boxing.

The phenomena of the world must be described and ordered before they can be brought into a theory. This is the very foundation of the dispensoric theory, which claims to seize the phenomena of the world in their totality. If one tries to apply this theory in education it means to substantiate a universal theory of education which in the last analysis is confirmed in practice. Here, practice has to be understood in its simple sense as individual and societal acting. Therefore the dispensoric theory of education is not only an epistemological principle, but above all, means orientation to act in order to change or transform individual and social conditions of life, which have the capacity to balance the cultural and social differences according to tendency.

(From Reyem 1980: 33, translation ours)

Wolfgang Meyer introduced the text to his students with a remark that it dealt with the latest educational theory. His suspicions were confirmed when in his lesson he discussed the objectives of the dispensoric theory, its anthropological background, its epistemological and philosophical implications and methods with his students. None of the senior secondary school students unmasked the text as meaningless. They all did the homework about the text without question.

Later, Meyer showed the text to a supervisor of students in teaching practice at his school who, because of his education and training, should have been capable of recognising the text as meaningless. His immediate responses signalled that he had already reached an advanced level in teacher training: 'interesting' – 'difficult abstract text' – 'which year?' – 'can be used in year 12'! This comment by an authority encouraged Wolfgang Meyer further. He passed the text on to other colleagues – with a stunning effect: nobody unmasked the dispensoric theory. A colleague who, as a student supervisor in teaching practice, prided himself on always being informed about the latest educational theories was apparently very impressed by the philosophical considerations of nature in the text. He thought the text was 'extremely interesting', particularly since it reminded him of the 'Communicative Theory'. Moreover, his professional background became apparent when he reflected on its use in classroom teaching. Another teacher trainer commented that he had recognised traits of the 'Compensatory Theory' in the text.

A couple of weeks later Wolfgang Meyer became convinced that there must be some method behind this imbecility. When a friend at the University of Cologne discussed the text with his students, the result was the same as at school: school pupils, university students, supervisors in teacher training and teachers all seem to be taken in by the mere surface appearance of 'science'. Of course, he realised that there were factors that exacerbated the problem, such as the social pressures caused by the situation, the need of some to produce something which is regarded by the others as clever, the naive respect for authorities in good faith, vanity and pomposity, as well as the fear of shame. However, these reasons did not seem to be sufficient to explain the abandonment of common sense.

Some English-speaking readers may be tempted to see the problem here as lying with the formality and authority of academic German prose, but consider the next example. This exercise was devised by Jack Sanger and we have used it in a number of classes as well as in distance teaching programmes. First, we ask people to carry out the following task:

> You have two minutes to read the story below, then turn the page and record against each statement TRUE (T), FALSE (F) or DON'T KNOW (D).

The story

A member of staff had just turned off the lights of the drama hall when a boy appeared and demanded equipment. The teacher unlocked the store cupboard. Contents of the store cupboard were grabbed and the boy raced off. A member of the senior staff was notified immediately.

Statements about the story

1 The boy appeared after the primary teacher had turned off the drama hall lights.
2 The robber was a boy.
3 The boy who appeared did not demand equipment.
4 The woman who unlocked the store cupboard was the teacher.
5 The teacher grabbed up the contents of the store cupboard and ran away.
6 Someone opened a store cupboard.
7 After the boy, who demanded the equipment, grabbed up the contents of the cupboard, he ran away.
8 While the cupboard contained equipment, the story does not say how much.
9 The robber demanded equipment of the teacher.
10 The robber opened the store cupboard.
11 After the drama hall lights were switched off, a boy appeared.
12 The robber did not take the equipment with him.
13 The robber did not demand equipment from the teacher.
14 The teacher unlocked a store cupboard.
15 The age of the teacher was not revealed in the story.
16 Taking the contents of the store cupboard with him, the boy ran out of the store.
17 The story contains a series of events in which only three persons are referred to: the teacher, the boy who demanded equipment and a senior member of staff.
18 The following events were included in the story: someone demanded equipment, a store cupboard was unlocked, its contents were grabbed up and a boy dashed out of the drama hall.

(Deakin University 1994: 22–3)

Almost everyone finds this task frustrating and confusing. It presents itself as a straightforward 'test' but quickly deconstructs if pursued in these terms. Next, though, we ask people to give 'the test' to others. Once in the teaching role most people feel confident and in control, quite the contrary to the feelings they had as a 'victim' (to use the word that they often use to describe themselves). Though the content is just as confusing they find the familiarity of the teaching role reassuring; some people even talk of it being enjoyable. Interestingly, given Meyer's experiment, they report that students, especially those in the later years of high school, are most likely to work through the task unquestioningly and will often start saying things like

'Oh, I know what this is' before beginning. Upper secondary school students are also the people who are best able to find 'yes' or 'no' responses (they have far fewer 'don't knows'), they have little or no interest in discussing the questions and seem only interested in knowing their 'score'. Our students also report that police officers and lawyers are among those who become most intently involved in this task!

It is tempting to read Meyer's study and Sanger's exercise as concerned only with the fallibility of human perception and memory but both have a greater significance. Remember that Meyer's study arose from his puzzlement that students appeared unmoved by a text that referred to Auschwitz, setting the content aside in order to reveal the algorithm that would generate a satisfactory answer in the context of the school curriculum. Again, we return to the cross cutting of issues that might at first appear discrete – the social nature of perception and the nature of social change.

THEORY, AUTHORITY AND EDUCATION

In contemporary societies, relationships between people seem to have become more and more problematic, while an unquestioned belief in science has forged ahead. This curious mix of growing social complexity and the simultaneous belief in simplified and unidimensional explanations for it is somewhat puzzling. In education, in particular, scientific reasoning has somehow missed its self-declared goal of reducing our dependence on an irrational authority associated with unthinking acceptance of the teachings of the Church. Science, which was once seen as the most effective means of combating irrational authority, has now assumed the myth of intellectual omnipotence.

The example of the dispensoric theory has dramatically shown the peak of absurdity that this can reach. Rather than legitimating all attempts to question, contemporary science seems sometimes to reduce our capacity for scepticism. There is of course a parallel in this apparent collusion between the nature of the dispensoric theory itself and the Fascism which was Meyer's starting point. His exercise demonstrates the ease of social acceptance of an absurd social theory given the authority inherent within the social organisation of research. In the end, Wolfgang Meyer had to admit that the dispensoric theory, despite his rejection of the echoes of Fascism, had left its mark on him too, since because of the reactions he received, he was in turn able to make his mark in the research literature as a theorist, thus closing the circle.

We have 'successfully' used the dispensoric theory of education in various research methodology classes in an attempt to deconstruct an unquestioning belief in the authority of 'theory'. Most students find a lot of arguments to justify the individual statements they make in support of

'Reyem's' text (Reyem, as you probably guessed, is Meyer spelt backwards), most of which they derive from accepted educational theories. Perhaps this suggests that even absurd theories can be treated as admissible because all theories seem absurd anyway. Perhaps it indicates the deep structuring of authority implicit in classes on theory taught by university professors. Whatever the reason, it seems that discussions of theory either invite the kind of uncritical flocking behaviour that shocked Meyer, or they invite heightened scepticism and, equally uncritically, rejection.

Incidentally, a similar deconstructive task to that developed by Wolfgang Meyer was used in the popular film *The Dead Poets' Society* by the charismatic English teacher John Keating. In his first class at a strict academy for boys he asked the students to tear out pages from the academic preface to their set book – an anthology of poetry. Rather than trick students into acceptance of an absurd theory in order to pass exams, John Keating invites students to destroy a text, which in the context of an English literature class is tantamount to sacrilege. But rather than release students from the discipline of poetry lessons in order to encourage them to seek out the poetic, the consequence is to mobilise institutional resistance to his theory.

Earlier we referred to the problem of 'abstraction'. Part of what abstraction involves is the use of theoretical language to create distance between the writer and reader. A distance which then becomes the basis for authority. Since theories are always abstractions from reality, they are usually presented to the reader as devoid of ownership, construction, time and place. Because of the resulting separations between subject and object, form and contents, a theoretical text creates a new 'reality', which gains fresh momentum when it is let loose among academic tribes and territories (Becher 1989). Students are often all but forgotten unless they too want to join the (increasingly competitive) academic race for tenure, promotion and a place in the pages of citation indicies. Bruno Latour comments, albeit with a jaundiced eye:

> Theories, now made abstract and autonomous objects, float like flying saucers above the rest of science, which by contrast becomes 'experimental' or 'empirical'. The worst is yet to come. Since sometimes it happens that these abstract theories, independent of any object, nevertheless have some bearing on what happens down below in empirical science – it has to be a *miracle*! . . . Speaking about theories and then gaping at their 'application' has no more sense than talking of clamps without ever saying what they fasten together, or separating the knots from the meshes of a net. Doing a history of scientific 'theories' would be as meaningless as doing a history of hammers without considering the nails, the planks, the houses, the carpenter and the people who are housed, or a history of cheques without the banking system.
>
> (Latour 1987: 242)

RESEARCH AND ME

One way of relating social theories more to the real world of human interactions, the constructing and organising process of knowledge and theorising, is to see the researchers included in, rather than outside, the body of their own research. The experience of the Elephant story in Chapter 2, of memory-work in Chapter 3 and the use of pictures in Chapter 4 have all shown that we can think of research as constituted by processes of individual and social reflexivity and reciprocity. In order to make them more aware of this relationship we have asked our students in different methodology classes how they see their research in relation to themselves. Here are three examples from a methodology class in peace education. We first asked each student to visualise what research means to them personally, so as to give each of them the chance to associate more freely than remaining restricted to using language as a 'prison house' (Haug *et al.* 1987). The first drawing was by Jürgen from Switzerland (see Illustration 11).

Jürgen gave the following commentary on his drawing:

> It looks like a . . . and to comment on the pictures, so I start at the sheet, it is my consciousness and there's somewhere a centre, what I know best, what is closest to myself, which is represented by the dark dot, and then this consciousness is expanding, covers different areas and has lost spots somewhere, not connected and the other is connected. There are also holes in that extended consciousness of things that are nowhere in the midst of my consciousness, of my knowing, or even the closest to the centre there are things that I do not know myself. So taking now this mind map, how I could call it, mind map of consciousness. Within this the research would be what I represented with those arrows, the expansion of consciousness of knowing in all directions connecting the different lost spots interconnecting knowing and also filling up the gaps which are the left-overs in the hurrying expansion. Well, that's about it.

In his drawing (Illustration 12), András symbolises the relationship between research and himself as a bridge. András is an anthropologist whose fieldwork was among the Romas (sometimes called 'gypsies' by those of us who know no better) in Hungary.

András commented on his drawing as follows:

> This is a bridge, a symbol of the bridge, it's a very dynamic, moving bridge and on one side, on the left side of the drawing that's the Roma national flag, and the Romas, at least according to my personal experience, would like to get integrated in society, in Hungarian society in all of

Illustration 11 Research and me: Jürgen

Illustration 12 Research and me: András

the senses one can imagine politically, mainly economically, but in other senses as well. And on the other side of the bridge, this big question mark is me. The only thing I'm really certain about is that I'm uncertain in a lot of senses. So this is a very personal view of the Hungarian society and since we are coexist – I mean I'm a non-Roma, so I'm not a member of the Roma community, but I feel the need to establish links and try to improve our coexistence within this society as much as possible, so I'm trying to do a lot of work, I'm involved in a lot of projects about them. But at the same time, so this is what the arrows towards the Roma community symbolize, but at the same time I always fear, and I'm aware of the impact that by using and by talking about them or by working with them I'm legitimizing myself, my own voice. And these are the arrows which are pointing back towards me, and sometimes these dilemmas, these doubts, these feelings are very strong, so I'm considering just stepping down from the bridge and these are the arrows which are pointing down from the bridge. So this is a very personal and political statement about research; how I feel research about the Romas. So there are two little shoes right next to the question mark and these are shoes without my feet in them so I really feel that the shoes should move the steps towards the Romas and, not towards the Romas, but with the Romas in a certain sense should be taken, but my feet are still not there because of the doubts I was just talking about, I just sometimes feel that this is just a means to legitimize my own voice. And now, just finally two words about the bridge: so it's a very personal view of Hungarian society, where it's just one segment of the society, in fact this is a very, it's hard to say, it's a very unstable bridge, it's filled up with stereotypes, it's moving all the time. You don't know if you begin to take the steps, maybe it's gonna collapse at one point. There were already anti-Roma events at Rosatits [place name] taking place in Hungary, so I'm not sure whether this bridge is the way, so whether you can really take steps on this bridge, but still it's there and so these shoes should be moving, but I'm . . . sometimes I don't know if my feet will be on those shoes but I really hope so.

The third drawing was by Onoriode from Nigeria (see Illustration 13). This is how Onoriode commented on her drawing:

This diagram symbolically shows how research has been part of my life. If you look at the diagram you have three, there are four . . . it just tries to tell that, you know, when on our own . . . we don't really know everything, or it's not possible for one person to know everything, there are always people who know more than you or who know the things you don't know. So naturally you need other people, like if you look at it, I have some, I have diagrams of some houses here. If one stays and just isolates oneself in one of these houses, and you don't know much and you don't bother to get your little shell to interact with other people in order to know what they know, because, I mean, it's certain that you need what other people know, you need other people's knowledge . . . if you just stay on your own, there is the likelihood you don't know everything, so there's the possibility of . . . and if you decide to

Illustration 13 Research and me: Onoriode

stay within . . . if you decide to remain ignorant there's the possibility of falling apart, but if you get out and get to interact with other people and add to your knowledge you naturally learn more to enable you [to] survive and this is like saying we live in an interdependent world and nobody can do it alone or go it alone. In essence, what I'm trying to say is that . . . no man is an island, we always need other people and we need to add other people's knowledge to our knowledge to be able to get . . . to be able to obtain something concrete or make sense at all of what is happening around us. If we take the example of the research . . . we did with the apple the first day you were here . . . three people touched different parts of the apple . . . but it never occurred to them to put the different findings together. I mean if they had done that they probably would have made sense to them that what they had looked like an apple . . . because they kept looking at everything in isolation they never put the three different parts or the three different perceptions together. They couldn't figure out that the object they had touched was an apple.

RESEARCH IS A SOCIAL (READ POLITICAL) ACTIVITY

These images and their interpretations reconnect and synthesise themes that recur in this book. We hear each voice attempting to validate the self as a resource for research in the context of social change. The issues of personal commitment, relevance, meaning and value that are raised by András, Onoriode and Jürgen might seem at first sight the very antithesis of research because, some will argue, they transgress a central value of research, which resides in the concept of 'objectivity'. What our examples provide, they might say, is vivid but it suffers from being subjective. The pieces we have quoted might also seem, in more subtle ways, the antithesis of what it means to theorise, for theory (even thought) is commonly thought of as being written, not spoken. We remind you however that in Chapter 3 we saw the fallibility of this view for the findings of collaborative memory-work have many echoes here.

In contrast, our view is that 'objectivity' is not an absolute value enshrined in the application of certain research procedures and practices but arises from the struggle to free oneself from prejudice and bias. Onoriode, András and Jürgen are all clearly struggling to see things clearly and to see themselves as part of the situations that they describe. 'Objectivity', here, is not a condition that can be assured by compliance with procedures, but an honesty and truth that can be achieved only by conscious critical effort and with difficulty. Randall Albury, who has looked more closely at this issue, has argued that none of the accepted commonsense definitions of 'objectivity' withstand scrutiny. In particular, he argues that the notion of objectivity as 'value-free knowledge' depends on adopting

> a whole host of values such as the value we place on empirical content, precision, testability, simplicity, elegance and so on;
>
> (Albury 1983: 15)

thereby invalidating any claim that such knowledge can be 'value-free'. Using as examples the disputes that arise between scientific experts who give conflicting judgements when called on to give evidence in environmental enquiries, Albury points out that this is an argument with important practical consequences:

> We are faced with more than an academic puzzle when our common-sense approaches to objectivity collapse. We are faced with the very practical problem of finding a basis for deciding between conflicting opinions on scientific and technical matters of major social significance.
>
> (Albury 1983: 18)

The opening up of scientific research to this kind of discussion is important because there is often a temptation to treat social research as a special case, deficient in its grip on objectivity when compared with science. The relation of theory and practice in social research often appears to present a thorny set of problems not so visible in other areas. In science, for instance, the relations that applied researchers have with theory are mostly distant and not seen to be of immediate consequence. For the most part the routines of data collection and analysis appear, at first sight at least, to be virtually automatic and free from controversy, and are validated and legitimated by the expertise and by the credentials of the researcher and his or her institutional affiliations. Only when unexpected complications occur, or when interest groups of one kind or another try to shift the definition of the problem on social grounds, does the objectivity of the research falter.

Think, for instance, of the disputes concerning research on the links between smoking and cancer, on the occupational hazards of working with asbestos or in radioactive environments, of studies of airport noise, industrial pollution or declining marine populations. When scientific research attempts to intervene in such areas of contentious debate, what tends to result is that discrepancies between findings and predictions press debate into close scrutiny of the methods, procedures and practices adopted by researchers. Indeed, faced with results or conclusions that are threatening, officials and others will often resort to attacks on method. This can turn the debate to technicalities, and press the researchers to the use of only those methods and techniques that seem most resilient to attack – often if only because they are technically complicated or abstruse.

Randall Albury argues that what is at stake in disputes over evidence provided by experts is the notion of objectivity itself:

> Whether it is used to defend government policy or to attack it, the argument we have been discussing rests upon a fundamental underlying assumption: that the resolution of a political dispute can in principle be treated as a technical problem of applying the appropriate objective knowledge and eliminating various forms of bias. But this assumption, in turn, presupposes that there is such a thing as unbiased, objective knowledge in the first place.
>
> It is for this reason that I think that the problem of objectivity in science has enormous social significance. Because science is the form of knowledge which, in our culture has the strongest claim to be objective; and if our present conception of the objectivity of expert advice on scientific and technological subjects can be brought seriously into question, as I think it can be, then the ground rules for political debate on a wide variety of matters must be radically altered.
>
> (Albury 1983: 8)

So, it would seem that the pursuit of scientific objectivity is no real solution to the problems that arise in social research, for objectivity itself, as Albury goes on to argue, is largely defined by powerful interests within scientific and research communities, and so is a part of, not outside, the political process, despite its professed desire to be so.

So why do we cling to the notion that we need theory in social research to protect us from political scrutiny? The heart of the problem appears to lie in the roles we assign to experts and their relation to those Jean Lave would term 'just plain folks'. Scientists (researchers) are reluctant to allow public participation in the research enterprise, keeping jpfs defined as 'subjects', in part because they fear that to allow active participation would threaten to dismantle the social structures and power relations that make the scientific enterprise possible. Instead, public participation is courted in the form of promises for the future and the promulgation of myths about science as our best guarantee of progress.

The consequence is that we cannot maintain distinctions between social and scientific research as qualitatively different. All research is inevitably in some sense a social activity and therefore involves political action. But there are more ways of enforcing a divide between experts and jpfs than differential allocation of roles and one of the most effective is jargon. The adoption of exclusive registers, arcane genres and specialised discourse are as effective as any other means in restricting access to research and, paradoxically, the arguments made by academics in favour of greater public participation are often most prone to cultural imperialism of this kind (as we have inadvertently demonstrated in this sentence alone).

Once we raise questions over the nature of objectivity and the need for abstraction, academic 'theory' takes on a different complexion. Rather than seeing academic theory as the peak of human knowledge – the ordered, abstracted and distilled essence of everything we know and know we know – it becomes best seen as the attic room of research. Academic theory is then characterised by nostalgia and redundancy, constituted by the discarded and neglected ideas and outmoded paraphernalia of forgotten thoughts, outgrown dreams and past aspirations: a source of ideas, not a warrant for them.

'THEORY' IN PRACTICAL RESEARCH

The collapse of faith in objectivity as a key to science opens the door to new approaches to social science, for 'subjectivity', locked for so long in the closet, can be taken out, dusted down and shaken into life. This is not just a technical issue for methodology but itself a significant change, reawakening questions about the uses and purposes of research, research practice and the nature of research knowledge which are at least as much ethical as they are technical. And, as we have constantly reminded ourselves, this changes the frames around what we consider personal and what we think of as social. Research itself is essentially a social activity, not somehow removed from and outside social life.

We need constantly to keep in mind the interrelated nature of theory and practice in relation to research. Theory might seem to stand in relation to research as a recipe to cooking, a dictionary to a text or a manual to software. But to think of it in this way is misleading, for theory is not just a back-up that can be turned to when all else fails, rather it is what makes it possible to see the world differently and so be able to act in different ways. Just as words make it possible to write, read, converse, lecture, persuade, debate, sing, argue, betray and seduce, so theory is concerned with giving meaning and intent to action, and with reading meaning and intent in the actions of others. Theory extends our capacity to see alternatives, reminding us of the lost opportunities we create with every action we take and every word we speak. Its concern is not simply to say why the world is as it is but to provide us with space to think how it could be different.

7 Emotional work in doing research: looking at/with a blind spot in academic relationships

Writing a piece of research means having fun, and doing the work is like slaughtering a pig, as the Italians say: 'You don't throw anything away.'
(Eco 1988: 265, translation ours)

NO FUN FOR THE PIG

We applaud Umberto Eco's sentiment, but of course something is lost — the life of the pig. And in research too, transposing raw data into meaty evidence means life is lost in the course of something new being created. Furthermore, as living culture is cut up to become research data, the researcher is the witness with blood on his or her hands. As there is guilt to be managed some grieving may be called for, but grieving cannot be done alone, it requires ceremonial.

The emotions involved in doing social research are rarely discussed, indeed it is only in the last ten years that researchers have seen the need to think about the ethical implications of their work, let alone its human impact. The asssumption seems to have been that the relationships between researchers and subjects, writers and readers, students and supervisors are based on some principle of rational behaviour that gives them a purity beyond exploitation or emotion. In the space of one chapter we cannot discuss the full range of questions this raises but we will focus on the particular circumstances of the relationships between students and supervisors. While this restricts the scope of this chapter it does reveal, sometimes in acute form, issues that will be present in any social research project. As is often the case, we find general issues about the practice of research surface most dramatically when overlaid by the particular authority structures that characterise student projects and the roles of supervisors. When the need is to manage the guilt that is a consequence of research undertaken as part of your studies for a degree, it is the supervisor's responsibility to manage the necessary ceremonies, though the grief remains your own.

A woman researching her dissertation on the writing of master's and doctoral theses once asked Michael if the students he supervised received the personal support (as opposed to academic support) that they needed to finish their research papers. Her question is significant, for it raises the whole issue of research itself being social action and not objectively disconnected from it. The practical questions this raises include the difficulties of managing field relations, which is a theme frequently discussed in the research literature, though usually in an instrumental rather than a personal way (for instance by Wax (1971), Norris (1977), MacDonald and Walker (1974), Hammersley and Atkinson (1983)). It also includes the limited, but troubling, questions about research relationships that are less often asked, such as how you stop once you have finished. For it is one thing to complete the thesis and collect the certificate but another to learn to live without it as a central fact of your life. (Similarly, in her novel *The Secret Lives of Eleanor Jenkinson*, Ann Oakley describes how 'the novel I am going to write' comes to play a central role in the life of her main character long before she writes anything at all.)

LIVING WITH THE PIG

A student once told us that she found herself unaccountably blocked in the final stages of completing the thesis. She knew that she had all the information she needed to finish it but for two years she would catch herself adopting all kinds of strategies to avoid closure. It took her time to realise that basically she did not want to finish. As she said, this was one of the few things she had done in her life that was her own. She found herself teaching other people's classes and other people's courses, acting as an assistant on other people's research (and almost always the other people were men). The thesis was hers and she did not want to lose it. She said that to complete it would feel like giving away a child. From an academic point of view the thesis was complete, but from a personal perspective it was not. What responsibilities does the supervisor have in such a situation? What ceremonies might manage the pain of such loss?

Research is sometimes thought of as a lonely and isolated enterprise (hours spent in the library learning facts so abstruse that there are only a handful of people in the world who will understand what it is you are saying). But involvement in social research inevitably means involvement in relationships, and often involvement of a peculiarly intense kind. Managing supervision (or any other aspects of the research process) requires a level of social skill, but to say this implies that such skills are a desirable but additional extra. We argue that, far from being extra, the relationships that are created between those implicated in a research project should have primacy when we discuss questions of methodology. We may mismanage such relationships, perhaps by default, but they exist, they are real and they are central to the process. They include not just field relations, but the relationships you have with your peers, with those you encounter in academic networks and with your supervisors. The idea that supervision can be adequately managed by recourse to recipe knowledge and might exist outside a personal relationship is clearly nonsense.

Like the life history of the butterfly, supervision takes place in a limited span of time, in a precious and fragile environment, it draws on a highly restricted source of nourishment and yet within it great changes have to be managed. Just when you come to terms with each stage – an initiation, a period of growth and transformation and an end – you find everything has changed. Sometimes the entries and exits to each stage are catastrophic. The relationships that make the process [im]possible, particularly the relationships between student and supervisor, are often critical.

A paradox is that most of us turn to social research because we are motivated by an interest in social change, yet frequently find this turmoil in our own lives unsettling. Most of us want to make the world a better place and becoming involved in research seems to be an appropriate, congenial and effective way to do this. But the changes actually brought about by social research are usually most acute for those who have most invested in the study, and almost always that means those who are doing the work. The very motivations we bring to research are often in danger of being corroded by doing it.

The strong boundaries that science has established between objectivity and subjectivity (originally to keep superstition at bay) means that altruism is the motive we will often display when presenting our face to the public. But altruism is increasingly difficult to sustain; perhaps when we are most vociferous in claiming that we do the work we do as a service to others, we are most likely to be striving to identify ourselves within it. An example that is more honest than most is Andrew Sparkes' life history of a PE teacher which implicitly and repeatedly tracks the route of research from intimacy to objectivity and back again, continually adjusting the extent of disclosure between researcher and subject, researcher and audience as it addresses the theme of homosexuality (Sparkes 1994). Often, it seems, we find ourselves researching topics that touch our personal vulnerabilities in ways that are not immediately obvious to us when we begin. To talk about our research is often to reveal our areas of greatest personal doubt.

To answer Michael's student, it is true that if we ask how somebody acquires the right to supervise research students, it is not usual to question the person's ability or skill in advising and supervising, but to look first at their research and publication record. Historically, the reasons for this are clearly related to the need of the university to protect freedom of expression without favour or prejudice. But an unintended consequence is that, despite the fact that enrolling as a graduate student in social research is to enter a high risk occupation, students may find themselves being viewed as a commodity in the academic market and working with supervisors who are busily competing in the hectic academic business of publishing or perishing. This does not promise well for the student's desire to act as an agent of social change. This structure, and the pressures it creates on people within it, leads to confusion and misunderstanding within which there may be little time for taking into account the student's personal concerns or holding the rope as they cross the chasm.

This is not to accuse supervisors of neglect, but to suggest that the situations in which supervisors and students find themselves put both in a bind, if not a knot. As Bob Connell remarks:

> The commonest complaint of PhD students is that they never get to talk to their supervisors. The commonest complaint of supervisors is that their PhD students never come to talk to them.
>
> (Connell 1985: 40)

But when students do see their supervisors, only certain of their concerns can usually be voiced. In many cases the time available restricts the supervisor to the most urgent aspects of the work in progress, so whatever fears or uncertainties the student tries to express, the chances are they will emerge from the supervisor's office holding yet another reading list. Indeed many of us manage the process of supervision by following every trail that the student signals to a suggested reading, and count that as success, for that is what we know about, that is our expertise.

If the student is to successfully orient the course they may need some collaboration or leadership. They will need time and support if they are to develop a personal voice, but those best placed to provide help – their supervisors – have become part of the academic system and as such are expected to act as elders in their disciplinary tribe (see Becher 1989). As a consequence, the student may feel caught between an idealised set of expectations being held out to them by what they read, and which they perceive as a measure against which they are expected to perform, and limited personal encounters with the immediate guardian of those ideals. Not surprising then if they experience a sense of alienation from the real world, as

> the individualism of academic language greatly underplays the extent to which the production of knowledge is a social process. Universities aren't located somewhere out in deep space. The problems intellectuals work on grow out of the society they live in (including its encounters with the natural world). The resources they have for working on those problems are socially produced. And often the solutions are implicit in,

or at least related to, the actions of people outside the academy who encounter the problems in a practical form.

(Connell 1985: 38)

In what we have said we need to guard against the seductive appeal of binary distinctions. It is tempting to see supervision as either a rite of passage requiring pain to be borne stoically if we are to be admitted to the tribe, or as concerned only with our personal development. Of course it is both, and more besides. One way of readjusting our perspective is to refer again to the diagram in Chapter 2 (Figure 1, p. 37) and address it in the form given in Figure 5.

It is clear that the work of a research student is not just that of making sense of some aspect of the social world that has not been closely studied before, since such work is only legitimate within the context of a particular

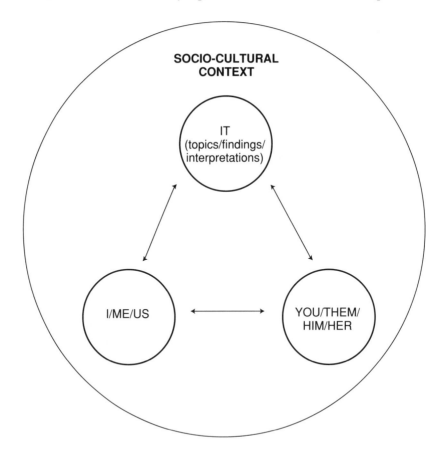

Figure 5 The context of research

set of relationships, at the heart of which stands (or more often sits) the supervisor, acting both as a gatekeeper to the discipline and as a teacher employed by the university. Doing research is work, and since both student and supervisor are caught up in the work of an organisation, their relationship is not just cognitive or even social, it involves feelings as well. As Stephen Fineman puts it in the opening paragraph of a paper that reinstates the need for consideration of emotions in organisational theory:

> Feelings shape and lubricate social transactions. Feelings contribute to, and reflect, the structure and culture of organisations. Order and control, the very essence of the 'organisation' of work, concern what people 'do' with their feelings.
>
> (Fineman 1993: 9)

Normally we conceive the work of both supervisor and student to be focused on the topic of the student's research, but it is rare for a relationship between two people to be so simple, especially when, as in this case, the student is at a turning point in their life and there is a great asymmetry in the distribution of power between the student and the supervisor. As Fineman says elsewhere in his paper:

> Our personal histories are not simply placed on hold, but are activated by, or in, the daily encounters of working.
>
> (Fineman 1993: 23)

STANDING TOGETHER AT THE THRESHOLD OF KNOWLEDGE

Academic rhetoric has it that supervisor and student stand side by side, their gaze fixed on the frontier of knowledge, which they imagine lies just a few steps beyond their present, perhaps precarious, position. It is the student's task to take a step beyond what the supervisor, and the field, know to be true. At some point in their progress together it is the student who has to go over the top. The supervisor may go first or may remain in the trenches so as to report progress, but however the action progresses both student and supervisor are well aware that the supervisor is in charge, and that his or her loyalty is as much to the regiment as it is to the troops.

Seen from within the scientific community, the supervisor must act (in the same way as the reviewers for academic journals often act) to protect their interests. As elders of the 'academic tribe' they have to defend their 'territories'. As Tony Becher describes:

The tribes of academe, one might argue, define their own identities and defend their own patches of intellectual ground by employing a variety of devices geared to the exclusion of illegal immigrants . . . their traditions, customs and practices, transmitted knowledge, beliefs, morals and rules of conduct, as well as their linguistic and symbolic forms of communication and the meanings they share. To be admitted to membership of a particular sector of the academic profession involves not only a sufficient level of technical proficiency in one's intellectual trade but also a proper measure of loyalty to one's collegial group and of adherence to its norms. An appreciation of how an individual is inducted into the disciplinary culture is important to the understanding of that culture.

In its very nature, being a member of a disciplinary community involves a sense of identity and personal commitment, a 'way of being in the world', a matter of taking on 'a cultural frame that defines a great part of one's life' (Geertz 1983). For a would-be academic, the process of developing that identity and commitment may well begin as an undergraduate, but is likely to be at its most intense at the postgraduate stage, culminating in the award of a doctorate and, for the chosen few, the first offer of employment as a faculty member.

(Becher 1989: 24–5)

But Becher describes only half of the process, the conformist half. True, there is always a strong element of conformity in supervision as the work of the student is bent and twisted to fit the templates of the discipline, but this almost always has its counterpart in resistance. In the stories students tell about supervisors there is a strong narrative element which celebrates the conflict of generations and competition for leadership of the tribe. Not surprisingly perhaps, relationships between tutors and students may be imbued with overtones of the conflicts and rivalries between children and parents, and sometimes with their displaced expression as sexual desire.

From one perspective Becher is right, and students do progress into conformity, but there should always also be a sense of the research degree as what Henry Giroux would call 'border pedagogy':

As a pedagogical process intent on challenging existing boundaries of knowledge and creating new ones, border pedagogy offers the opportunity for students to engage the multiple references that constitute different cultural codes, experiences and languages. . . . Within this discourse, students should engage knowledge as border-crossers, as people moving in and out of borders constructed around co-ordinates of difference and power. These are not only physical borders, they are cultural borders historically constructed and socially organised within rules and regulations that limit and enable particular identities, individual capacities, and social forms. In this case, students cross over into realms of meaning, maps of knowledge, social relations, and values that are increasingly being negotiated and rewritten as the codes and regulations that organise them become destabilised and reshaped.

. . . Border pedagogy shifts the emphasis of the knowledge/power relationship away from the limited emphasis on the mapping of domination toward the politically strategic issue of engaging the ways in which knowledge can be remapped, reterritorialised, and decentred. . . . students must be offered opportunities to read texts that both affirm and interrogate the complexity of their own histories. They must also be given the opportunity to engage and develop a counter discourse to the established boundaries of knowledge.

(Giroux 1992: 29–30)

THE POLITICS OF RESEARCH

The circle around the triangle in Figure 5 symbolises the socio-cultural framework within which supervision takes place. This, of course, also applies to the political context within which all research work is commissioned, planned, completed, reported, used and evaluated. Becher would have us take this context as given, a set of rules, practices and procedures to be adhered to, celebrated and followed; Giroux would insist both that the context be included in the research and that it be interrogated. But both Becher and Giroux, clearly coming from different perspectives, would agree that political issues are endemic.

Despite, perhaps because of, its avowed objectivity, social research can easily become both a vehicle and a target for political attack. The following letter which Michael received was in response to an evaluation report on cultural activities organised by teachers in Austrian schools. It was carried out by a student whose work he was supervising and provides a good example of the political process crossing to research ground in order to attempt a pre-emptive strike in the face of information it sees as politically sensitive:

On page 86 of the evaluation report you present the special situation in the Tyrol, where it reads: 'The schools cannot freely decide on certain projects which arise out of the needs of the individual school and have them financially secured.'

This statement is wrong and entirely unfounded. For years the TKS [Tyrolean Cultural Service] has supported more than 150 school-based projects every year, which were also financed if it was agreed on beforehand. Of course, each school can independently decide on what it chooses from our offer if it thinks this relevant for its situation and if it suits its needs.

The wrong statement quoted above and the tendency of the whole contribution derived from it are likely to damage the reputation of the TKS, its staff and the sponsoring agency, the Province of Tyrol.

The interview fragments quoted in the report, which are used as evidence, are anonymous, so it is not possible to verify them.

All this leaves the impression that here scientific exactness, objectivity and fairness have been negligently violated.

I therefore ask you to take an immediate step in correcting the text in its necessary range and within the framework of the circulation of the report.

(Translation ours)

Giroux would see this a border incident, since this is government applying pressure and challenging research to defend itself at what it takes to be a weak point. The likely sequence of defence and counter attack is fairly predictable, as Sir Humphrey Appleby (in the BBC television series 'Yes Minister') explains as he outlines the strategy to his Minister:

There is a well-established government procedure for suppressing – that is, not publishing – unwanted reports . . .

Stage one: the public interest
1) You hint at security considerations.
2) You point out that the report could be used to put unwelcome pressure on government because it might be misinterpreted.
3) You then say that it is better to wait for the results of a wider and more detailed survey over a longer time-scale.
4) If there is no such survey being carried out, so much the better. You commission one, which gives you even more time to play with.

Stage two: Discredit the evidence that you are not publishing
This is, of course, much easier than discrediting evidence that you *do* publish . . . You say:
(a) that it leaves important questions unanswered
(b) that much of the evidence is inconclusive
(c) that the figures are open to other interpretations
(d) that certain findings are contradictory
(e) that some of the main conclusions have been questioned.
    Points (a) to (d) are bound to be true. In fact all of these criticisms can be made of a report without even reading it. There are, for instance, always *some* questions unanswered. . . . As regards (e), if

some of the main conclusions have not been questioned, question them! Then they have.

Stage three: Undermine the recommendations
This is easily done, with an assortment of government phrases:
(a) 'not really a basis for long-term decisions . . .'
(b) 'not sufficient information on which to base a valid assessment . . .'
(c) 'no reason for any fundamental rethink of government policy . . .'
(d) 'broadly speaking, it endorses current practice . . .'
These phrases give comfort to people who have not read the report and who don't want change – i.e. almost everybody.

Stage four: If stage three still leaves doubts, then Discredit the Man who Produced the Report
This must be done OFF THE RECORD. You explain that:
(a) he is harbouring a grudge against the government
(b) he is a publicity seeker
(c) he is trying to get his knighthood
(d) he is trying to get his chair
(e) he is trying to get his Vice-Chancellorship
(f) he used to be a consultant to a multinational company *or*
(g) he wants to be a consultant to a multinational company.

(Lynn and Jay 1981: 258–9)

Locating the conflict on a border between the university and the outside may reduce the power gradient between supervisor and student and create the basis for collaboration, or at least for collusion. If the line of conflict is drawn between the student and the faculty this can be much more difficult to manage as both parties are expected to share values. If there is conflict within the process, the ground on which the student stands is within the territory of the tribe against which she or he must defend it.

The degree to which political issues saturate the research process is not always understood, especially by those directly involved. Within each research community, research methods and techniques are often thought of as merely technical, as 'instruments', but this is never the case. Values are close to the surface in even the most systematised process, though those closest to the process are usually the last to recognise them as such. Research questions are always embedded in a wider epistemological context, as are the researcher(s) and the supervisor(s). Epistemology is not simply logical; it is essentially ideological:

Epistemology provides a context in which to consider the rules and standards by which knowledge about the world is formed, the distinctions and categorizations that organize perceptions, ways of responding to the world, and the conception of 'self'.

(Popkewitz 1991: 15)

Since social action is always to be located in the wider context of the social, cultural and political domain, so, too, viable research methods are only possible in the context of a particular epistemology, even if this is taken for granted, which to some degree it always is and has to be.

EPISTEMOLOGICAL SHIFTS

Patti Lather (1991: 91) identifies three recent simultaneous epistemological shifts in research methodology. The first shift is away from an emphasis on general theorising to problems of interpretation and description. Lather argues that description/interpretation inevitably involves bringing to the fore one's own perspectivity. This presents a challenge to conventional views of objectivity. Can the voice of the researcher be anything but an intrusive voice? How do we include ourselves within the text and explore our reasons for doing the research without risking lapses into self-indulgence? Can we maintain the necessary commitment to the topic if we insist on putting ourselves at the centre?

The second shift refers to 'the textual staging of knowledge', which represents the attempt to give the original voices of those implicated in the research more room. Patti Lather is rightly critical of a strong convention in much qualitative research in which direct quotations from interviews are clipped and framed to suit the purposes of the researcher but often ripped from their context and source of meaning. Lather suggests we should follow original texts and be disciplined by them, rather than manipulate them to suit our own ends.

Turning the text into a display; developing narrative rather than narration; allowing interaction among perspectives; and presenting material rich enough to bear re-analysis in different ways – all this has serious implications for the reader. For rather than requiring the reader to be the passive recipient of univocal authority, it brings the reader into the analysis. In this sense the final text is incomplete for its validity has first to be tested against the reader's experience. Such writing requires the reader to probe blind spots in the researcher's conceptualisations and requires that the reader attends critically to all the constitutive elements of the study, not to just a few selected findings.

The third shift Patti Lather identifies is towards a focus on the social relations of the research act itself. Since the relations among the people involved mediate the construction of knowledge, this process has a political moment. Therefore the results achieved in the research process must always be read against an analysis of movements in power among the people involved. This requires that the reader has access to information about the relationships between individual researcher(s) and the other members of the research group on the one hand and their individual and collective interactions with the other people involved in the research process, such as the supervisor, on the other. This implies that an account of the process and practice of supervision should be included in the thesis, so that the reader is better able to judge the work of the student.

It is, of course, a difficult line to traverse. Discussions among researchers about the notion of objectivity are almost always conducted in terms of what is best for research, never what is best for the subject. Once we collapse the boundary between being inside research and being on the outside, we risk colonising the world of the 'subject' in new ways, not least by seeming to make our concerns seem more important than theirs, or by attempts to create an 'us' that is implicitly ethnocentric and essentially patronising. Lather is right that there are narrative dangers in conventional qualitative studies, not least being the common implicit assumption of the author as hero. The danger in post-structural writing is not so much a continuation of the irritating myth that the author is always right but the assumption that nothing is important unless it enters the consciousness or touches the sensibilities of the author.

But a stab of conscience tells us that you are awake enough to have read the last paragraph and turn it back on us. Ouch!

Perhaps either way the problem is essentially the same, in that what is at stake is a sense of trust between author and reader. Quite how such trust is constructed has not often been considered by social scientists (though as a bizarre social phenomenon it warrants study). Clifford Geertz's (1988) eloquent analysis of the writing styles of key figures in anthropology is probably the best example we have available.

WEARING THE COATS WE WEAVE FOR OTHERS

Geertz's message is that, despite the vagaries of human motivation, commitment and intent, the only instrument we have for social research is the human voice, albeit transformed into print (more recently Trevor Barnes and James Duncan (1992) have applied the same argument to geography). And perhaps this is the real challenge that students face, first to find their own voice within/despite the research community (and the university) and then to understand why this voice is as it is. Understanding one's own voice and why it is as it is requires an undestanding of its social context, which in turn prompts questions about history, biography and the socially situated nature of social action. Collaborative memory-work shows this clearly. We cannot understand who we are except through social action, and we cannot engage in such action without inviting change. None of us is an island entire. Ursula Schneider captures what we are trying to say exactly:

> What effect has the academic culture and the world of thought which I am confronted with at university? Which marginal, which crucial changes have occurred in the way I interpret the world? How do I experience academic culture: gowns, rites of initiation and exit, heroic myths, behaviour in discussions, opening to and closure from the outside world, above all abstractions and scientific language?
>
> How does this affect my own development, my attitude towards learning, science, social responsibility, my way of thinking and acting, my relationship to people outside higher education?
>
> Which highlights are there? What has bored me, made me excited, irritated, frustrated, enjoyed, hurt and why? Which theories can I make friends with? How do I select appropriately, where do I get lost? etc.
>
> It is a matter of reflecting one's own relationship to scientific thinking in the institutionalized setting of the university and a matter of testing theories for the usefulness for one's own means. These means can only be judged by oneself, and to do so is helpful in order to make one's own expectations and one's own entrance to theory explicit.
>
> (Schneider 1988: 81, translation ours)

We enter research training in order to become 'researchers' – respected members of the research community – but if we are to do research out of an interest in or commitment to social change there comes a point where we must break the community rules. Paradoxically, to negotiate this tight-rope skilfully is to be applauded by the research community (or it leads to being violently and publicly criticised, which is an even greater accolade). Initially we see the task of becoming researchers in the terms that Tony Becher describes, involving us in learning and learning to conform to the rules, customs and traditions in our chosen field. But when it comes to doing research we learn, sooner or later, that we have to break free of these same conventions if we are to be able to say anything that will bring about change. Perhaps this is like adolescents who in order to become individuals within the family have first to assert their independence of it.

Dan Bar-On, the Israeli Jew who interviewed the children of Germans who had carried out atrocities in the Death Camps, describes in gripping detail the process of coming to terms with this paradox. In the many interviews he carried out, and in some cases avoided, he was constantly faced both with controlling his own feelings and those of his subjects. As he fought to push all this material into generalisations, theory or explanation, he came to realise that much of what he had done, and what he knew as a result, defied such closure. In concluding an account of the method-ological process, he wrote:

I began writing articles about the working-through process. I was in the mood for summarising. But when I had finished the articles and given them to a few of my colleagues, their comments again gave the feeling that I had missed something. I was still trying to be the researcher, this time looking not for variables that correlate significantly but for patterns that emerge out of the data. It was still too difficult for me to present the interviews as raw data, to let readers crystallise their own concepts or conclusions. Only after going over the interviews for the third time did I finally decide to write a book in which readers would be their own researchers. Even then my valuable readers still had to edit out my emotionally loaded or analysing comments again and again. I had to 'let go' of the *researcher* in me completely and let the *person* who was part of the encounters speak freely. This was for me, extremely exposing, tearing away all the previous 'coats' I had wanted to put on this material, on myself.

(Bar-On 1991: 339)

Dan Bar-On's research takes as its subject extremes of human behaviour (though we shouldn't let this allow us to marginalise it), but the crisis he describes is one we all face in some form. If our concern is with research in the context of social change, we must also wear the coats we weave for others. In any social research project we must always develop our capacity to look within ourselves as we look out to others. As Sears (1992: 155), quoted by Sparkes, puts it, 'As we peer into the eyes of the other, we embark on a journey of the Self: exploring our fears, celebrating our voices, challenging our assumptions, reconstructing our pasts.' For Dan Bar-On the journey was particularly perilous, but this is no reason to dismiss it as exotic. The memories he released and the fears he encountered were clearly difficult to control, but the interplay between biography and social interaction and the need to control his own honesty amplify features of all social research. Mobilising subjectivity in research is not simply a technique to be used as a counter to objectivity, but opens doors to dark places and once you embark on the journey of self-discovery there is no telling where it might lead. Emotion is not a side effect or a pathological consequence of engaging in research; it is central to the project.

Being members of the research community gives us a licence to practice but it does not in itself provide the personal resources of motivation, commitment, reflexive capacity, intellectual skill or courage that we require if we are to do research. Indeed if we become over-socialised into the community we will probably lose any capacity we had to do so. Gill Plummer takes up this point in a paper in which she reports a sequence of letters between Kerry Newman, Richard Winter and herself. The issue revolves around an aspect of supervision we have been discussing here –

the politics of supervisor–student interaction. Gill opens the account with a letter she writes to Richard following a lunchtime conversation:

> Our conversation has stayed in my mind. I am a little disturbed by our lunch-time chat. It is difficult for me to know exactly what is the root of my anguish so this note is an explanation. I sense it is about issues of power. My feelings (these feelings are not realities) tell me it is to do with rejection.

But she does not finish the letter, and does not send it, for fear of hurting Richard's feelings. Instead she discussed it with women friends. First with Isobel:

> I was not a 'little disturbed' I was raging and clearly issues of trust had emerged. Remarking on 'these feelings are not realities', she [Isobel] asks, 'In what sense are they "not truth"?' Clearly I feel guilty. 'What have you crossed out?', she asks inquisitively. I'm silent but think this is the most pertinent question of all.

Later, in explaining the incident in a letter to Kerry, Gill writes:

> That afternoon [following the conversation with Richard] I felt slightly depressed; by the evening I felt rage, pure rage, and I raged and raged for days. I know from experience if I rage it's raising insecurities in me.

Gill then sends her letters to Richard, who replies:

> I suppose I am aware of the pain tutors can cause by rejecting a student's work when they impose their own conceptions rather than working out from where the student is 'at'. . . . I am shocked that you felt 'put down' (but I see your point, indeed). . . . Perhaps there is an issue here about the difference between the sort of responsibilities you feel towards a friend and as a professional.
>
> (Plummer *et al.* 1993: 310–13)

Gill Plummer, her friends and colleagues are clearly practised and accomplished writers who can express their feelings and their ideas clearly and directly in what they write. They have a high degree of control over their expression: writing seems to be their natural element. For them, writing is not just a way of recording things but a medium in which they can extend themselves. This is something most of us have to learn, and as we do so our efforts may falter, mislead or confuse, but this should not prevent us from beginning.

As well as using reflective forms of writing as a response after the event, writing can be used to create a structure of expectation and this may be a good way to begin. Michael regularly asks students to begin the process of supervision by entering a correspondence in which they express their expectations of him, and he replies. This has several advantages, not least that it establishes from the start that there are at least two viewpoints from which to interpret and understand what is happening in the supervision process. Also it creates a record where one might not otherwise exist. This can be helpful in negotiating a contract between supervisor and student but also in establishing a methodological model for supervision which may model the research process.

Establishing a correspondence shows clearly how the act of recording a social interaction changes things. The letters freeze what has been said, bring some questions to the fore and push others into the background, confuse 'objective data' and 'subjective interpretation', blend description and analysis, interpretation and evaluation. That these will be questions for the research project as well as for supervision can be helpful in understanding the research process. It is clear, for instance, that after an exchange of letters like the one that follows, the interaction between student and supervisor will change, the text of their interaction being read against the text of their correspondence.

The first letter is from Justine to Michael, at the start of the supervisory relationship. Michael's reply follows.

Dear Michael,

I have just noticed that my typewriter seems to be on strike – therefore this is going to be an authentic personal letter. I hope you can read my handwriting.

Here is what's important for our cooperation:

Time
It is important for me to have the feeling that I have enough time to get my ideas across. I tend to get under the pressure of time or I get the feeling that I am unjustifiedly taking away somebody else's time. I would rather we met a couple of times less often but had more time when we did meet. I think it would be helpful for me if we could decide before we meet how much time we need for each meeting: then I could better structure the time and adjust to it.

Perhaps you noticed yourself on Monday that I tend to just start talking quickly and without a real concept.

I have been brooding over this page for a while and nothing else comes to mind. This is probably an expression of my difficulties in recognising and expressing my own needs. I seem to be better at finding out about other people's needs and responding to them.

Encouragement

My way of working, particularly in the actual writing of academic work, has always been accompanied by setbacks as a result of my insecurity and lack of self-confidence (What do I know that's worth writing about?) on the one hand and high expectations of myself on the other. One of the things that has been very important for me so far has been that Helga [a colleague at the department] has given me the feeling that there is a lot, well almost anything, I can draw out from *myself*. Whatever I get from there is worth something. The help I get from outside cannot be the product itself, but rather provides guidance in finding out how to get something out of myself and how I can successfully transfer it. It has helped me a lot to (re)discover that I can/may be productive/creative and to find out that scientific work need not be grey and dusty. Something which had been covered up has come to the fore again, has started flowing once more . . . .

That's why I would not like to 'give up' Helga and hope it is possible for the three of us to work together. I'll talk to Helga about it. We both have already thought about what role my unending conflict with Mum and Dad plays here . . . .

Criticism/suggestions

are important to me and to my motivation. I think I can accept criticism quite well and I am learning not always to take critical comments of my work personally but rather to try to use them constructively. I am suspicious of the idea of cooperation without criticism.

Openness

What I mean here is that it is not only my research work that is the object of our cooperation, but WE, our relationship as well. It may become part of the topic and perhaps even should . . . .

I don't think I need to mention this to you.

Moreover, I will have a say in voicing my expectations – I don't want to withdraw from this responsibility. I hope I'll succeed in doing so. In this sense, I trust in both an enjoyable and successful cooperation.

Yours,
Justine

Some days later, Michael replied:

Dear Justine,

I have already been carrying your letter with me for a couple of days – from the university to my house, from there back to the university and so forth. I intended to answer your letter immediately, but now another couple of days have passed, although I'd meant to sit down right away and answer your letter.

I'm glad that it became an 'authentic personal letter', as it gave me more feeling of immediacy than it might have had. I was also very impressed that you reacted so quickly after our first meeting – and in such an extensive and differentiated way! I find it inappropriate that I'm sitting at the computer writing back to you but it has the great advantage that you don't have to bother about my handwriting which is difficult to decipher. But this is an excuse . . . so let me turn to the topics you raise in your letter:

I too find it important to pay attention to the time we have available, and I realise that I don't have as much time available as I would wish. I never thought this would happen to me but the 'Grey Men' do not stop in front of the university (have you read Michael Ende's book *Momo*?). To me Momo's way of looking at time is interesting since it sets itself visibly apart from 'Kronos time'. Let's introduce 'Momo time' for our meetings, then you don't have to have the feeling of stealing time from me.

Incidentally, where does this feeling of yours come from, since the time thieves are actually the Grey Men? Perhaps we could talk about this some time. As far as I'm concerned I expect to find the time with you stimulating because I will learn from you – and I do hope you won't miss this chance of learning from me . . . .

You want to have the feeling of having enough time. To begin with let's simply arrange the time which you think is necessary and let's see how we get on with it. Incidentally, I found our Monday meeting anything but 'talking quickly without a real concept'. I thought your suggestions were stimulating and exciting – did you not feel the same way?

I have just reached the part of the letter where you come to a standstill and write: 'This is probably an expression of my difficulties in recognising and expressing my own needs. I seem to be better at finding out about other people's needs and responding to them.' This is an attitude which will be very important and helpful for your professional work, but why didn't you apply it in our discussion (on Monday)? Later on you mention your 'unending conflict with Mum and Dad'. Do we/do you need an external model for explaining the relationship with your supervisor?

Although I have known you for only a short time, you appear to be a very committed and competent woman, able to stand firmly on her own feet; perhaps more firmly than many others who move on this parquet. I don't see Helga's role as one you need to consider 'giving up', but as an enrichment, but I'd also like to talk about this and what it might mean to all of us. Here Momo can have her first real test.

I want to comment on your 'setbacks of insecurity and lack of self-confidence'. I have the feeling – at least from my restricted view and from a male perspective – that you are very competent and confident and I believe that you can achieve a lot in your professional work, as you outlined it last time. As I said before, I can learn a lot from you, and therefore I'm happy that you have approached me about the supervision.

I have reached another important point in your letter where you mention openness. You have expressed my thoughts too when you stress that we should thematise our relationship. Without that, I think, it will be very difficult to get somewhere with your work. I'm happy that you see this the same way. I think that this will be a strength of your research and of our cooperation (I envisage the 'WE' as an important word). You end your letter hoping that we'll succeed in this and the 'trust in both an enjoyable and successful cooperation', without which I wouldn't like to cooperate at all.

Well, Justine, my eyes have just caught the colourful rainbow on your stationery. It simply ends on the right-hand side, as if we should find our future work there.

I'm looking forward to hearing from you about your first experience in the field,

Yours,
Michael

(Translation ours)

There are several good reasons for using letter writing as a way of starting off the supervision process. The most important reasons are as follows:

- Despite (or perhaps because) of the ubiquitous presence of modern telecommunication, letter writing still provides some private space for personal written communication.
- Personal letters are located in time. They have the potential to create shared memories, since they mark the distance travelled in the progress of a relationship.
- Since letters are exchanged between a particular 'sender' and 'receiver', they offer one of the few protected contacts between supervisors and students in these times of the mass university.
- Letters can offer neutral space, more so than the supervisory encounter which takes place in the supervisor's office. According to how they are answered, letters offer one of the few chances for supervisors and students to communicate on an approximately equal footing.
- In their informal character, letters contrast with the conventional text

types used in academic work, so giving student and supervisor an opportunity to step outside the formal genres and registers of academe and to comment on it in a different voice.

- Letters do not immediately call for assessment or rating in the way that student writing usually does when read by the supervisor.
- Students often find it easier to write down their thoughts, wishes, fears and expectations on their own rather than expressing them orally in the presence of a 'person of authority'. Additionally, the writer can edit the text before it is read, or decide not to send it at all, so providing a space for editorial control that is missing in face-to-face conversation.
- The writer can choose the time and the place when and where he or she writes a letter. This may help capture the right mood, or nuance of criticism, reproach or plea for reassurance.
- Letters allow the writer to some degree to control his or her presentation of self, which helps students include autobiographical experiences, and test new personae, in the process of knowing and understanding their research field.
- Letters provide a record of supervision which records at least two voices, a record that is difficult to recreate in hindsight and might otherwise be lost.
- Letter writing can model important aspects of the research process that are otherwise difficult to teach, especially the recording of field notes.
- Letter writing has proved to be a valuable instrument for receiving informal feedback in seminars and courses (cf. Plummer *et al.* 1993 and Schratz 1992).

END NOTE

We began this chapter with a recognition of the guilt that has to be managed in all social research, perhaps in all research, but we quickly eluded the question by refocusing on the emotions involved in supervisor–student relationships, returning only to the opening issue in considering Dan Bar-On's research. This might seem to be a way of avoiding questions we all find difficult but only if we take the view that the relationship between supervisor and research student is based on an apprenticeship model. If we take Giroux's notion of 'border pedagogies' seriously, then it is the work of the student that must be given centre stage, for the cutting edge lies here, not in the established traditions and conventions of the research community.

Furthermore, there is a tension between the university and the research community which we had not identified clearly before, and in which the supervisor is inevitably caught. The university, as a teaching institution, has one set of responsibilities to students, and as a research institution, another set of responsibilities to the invisible college. The student, too, has to conform to one set of expectations to gain entry to the research community, but realise other, often contradictory capabilities if he or she is to do social research. It might seem that action research can afford to ignore these issues, locating itself outside the academy and therefore free from the traditions and conventions that beset the supervision of research degrees. Perhaps so, though our experience is that action research can sustain itself only for so long out in social space. Most often it finds itself out on an umbilical or needing to return at intervals to replenish consumable resources and patch the space suit.

The emotions of supervision, we have come to realise, are not superficial but endemic and structural. They are a part of the politics of research, not apart from them. As we write this, looking out at the Tyrolean mountains from Michael's window, they seem to us more like the glaciers than the snow on the ground, for they are an integral and causal part of the structure of the landscape, not merely sprinkled on top of it.

8 In place of work: beyond the recognition of prior learning

Implicit in much of what we have said has been the assumption that we need to rethink social research in response to the changing nature of work and the workplace. In Chapter 1 we claimed that more and more of us find ourselves working in the information economy, dealing with the creation, management, evaluation and distribution of knowledge in one form or another. Working with knowledge implies that the work we do has a research dimension, even though this potential may not be fully realised in practice. And increasingly, access to knowledge, and the means to create it, determines the social structure. Those who are powerless in terms of information are the disadvantaged – the 'new' poor – and this creates the basis for continuing a tradition of social research begun by those nineteenth-century researchers who documented poverty in London, Berlin and elsewhere. When we do research, for whom do we do it? Who gains and who loses? What difference does our research make to who knows what about whom and when? In this chapter we will return to considering the nature of contemporary work as a theme, looking more closely at the question of research in relation to the increasing numbers of us whose work is in some way a part of the information economy.

In Australia and parts of Europe there is, as we write, an administrative vogue for the 'recognition of prior learning'. In practice this is usually taken to mean taking into account the full range of formal and informal learning someone has acquired when they apply to be admitted to a course of education or training. Less obviously, 'RPL' raises curriculum questions which are less frequently discussed and even more rarely practised, for to 'recognise prior learning' is to recognise the individuality of experience rather than searching for some form of common currency in order to calculate a common value for different forms of qualification.

While 'recognising prior learning' is an issue for all teachers, it becomes especially acute in courses beyond the initial training level, where it becomes clear that in some respects that are directly relevant to the curriculum, the student knows more than the teacher. To give just one example, in the master's degree unit on Classroom Research, which Rob teaches at Deakin University, of the twenty or so people who enrol, as many as half the group do not work in conventional school teaching. In the last few years those in other kinds of educational work have included nurses and nurse educators, those working in government or private training schemes, instructors in the police and the military, church people, people who run health centres, run restaurants, write computer software, work as consultants and advisers, work in museums and art galleries as well as a professional sportswoman and several musicians. Indeed, the variety of experience that people bring to the unit has caused us (the unit is taught jointly with Helen Modra) to rethink what we mean by a 'classroom', a question that has rebounded on us, as this is a distance course taught to students who may be working anywhere in the world and whom we rarely 'meet', at least in the conventional sense of being able to interact in temporary face-to-face proximity.

Like others facing similar diversity of experience among our students, we first responded by searching for common ground. We tried to construe the curriculum in such a way that people could navigate through it using as a reference point what it was in their work that was 'teaching' and the ways in which the work they did was educational. To begin with this seemed to work well, but after two years we found we had created our own clichés, and found too that we were not listening carefully when students retold us what we had told them. Our initial solution to the problem, of trying to create common ground from which the course could depart, proved to be problematic. It led us to an over-dependence on methodological recipes, of the kind of action research encountered when people took the action research spiral to be not an heuristic but a formula.

In our course, there came a point when the diverse experience of the group overtook us, when questions about content could not easily continue to be ignored or categorised in solely process terms, when the questions we were asking of them were ones we had also to ask ourselves. At this point, we had to reconstitute the course, and as part of this process we saw that as well as 'recognising prior learning' at the point of entry, we had also to consider this diversity of experience as central to the curriculum. Indeed, we began to think of the curriculum as being only partially defined by what we said to them, and more completely described by their work in response to what we asked them to do, seen in the context of an understanding of their workplace, their lives and careers.

This story has its parallels in the conceptual structure of this book, since we argued initially for a similar response to the problem of writing a book for an audience whose interests in education, and in research, we took to be multi-faceted and varied. We began by claiming to recognise diversity of experience, and then promptly proceeded to write as if we all shared a common background of experience and concern for research. By now the stresses endemic in this rhetorical formulation are probably beginning to show and you are looking for ways to respond more actively to the text.

EDUCATION AS DESKILLING

In the previous chapter we discussed the issue of academic supervision. Underlying this discussion was the assumption that the key to understanding the relationship between student and supervisor lies in finding ways to question the unchallenged expertise of the supervisor (the 'blind spot' in the language of the Johari window, to which we will refer in Chapter 9). Normally, this expertise derives from credentials that the supervisor has collected by scholastic performance somewhere in the obscure recesses of the academic disciplines.

The conventional relationship between student and supervisor, based on the assumption that the supervisor has access to privileged, not to say sacred, knowledge (the arcane tribal knowledge of the elders, Becher might say), is becoming less and less tenable. As the university moves to accept and develop its role, not just as a museum of learning but as an agent of social change, so it has to accept the shift in its measures of quality from an emphasis on publication to a concern with educational process. This is a shift that calls for a different conception of expertise, other ways of looking at what counts as research and new forms of relationship with its students, with its community and with the world at large. Currently, we can see universities developing different kinds of responses in the face of these concerns, including gross corporatism, the unseemly and uncritical embrace of the free market or the military–industrial complex and exotic forms of neo-colonialism, as well as occasional engagement in the serious educational issues that are involved. More often than not the university mission involves some cocktail of these survival strategies, as illustrated by Stewart Brand in his account of the work of the Media Lab at MIT (Brand 1987).

We mention this crisis of identity in the contemporary university because it provides some background to the issues we want to discuss, but this analysis of education policy/politics is not one we want to pursue. Our concern in this chapter is with the practical consequences of accepting a view of education as an area of practice defined by the very different interests and concerns that our students bring with them to the university when they come to learn about research. Recourse to our training in the closely demarcated territories that mark the academic rookeries may offer necessary, but certainly not sufficient, intellectual resources to help us.

The idea of inducting students into the closed traditions of the tribes that Tony Becher describes is no longer a tenable solution to our educational problem. In a period of multiplex social and cultural change, *recognising* prior learning may be exactly the wrong thing to do: more important may be to recognise people's capacity to unlearn (and perhaps, correspondingly, our capacity to unteach). Moreover, the curriculum context which makes recognition of prior learning possible is, in many areas, eroded and fragmented; the culture of academe is itself changing and in many areas the tribe has abandoned its caves and tunnels in the far recesses of the research literature and joined the migrating herds in search of new ways of life. In particular, those of us in education faculties who have pursued the changes of the last twenty-five years have seen what sometimes appear to be herd-like movements away from the empiricist dustbowl onto the wide plains of case study and action research. We have followed the migrations of qualitative method into the unfamiliar landscape of post-modernity and have seen the boundaries between the old tribes dissolve, sometimes to reform in camps that are surprisingly hostile to one another. Now looking out, rather than down, from our ivory (more often redbrick or fibro) towers we have watched (and encouraged) schools and school systems to change, sometimes carrying the banners of change ourselves, but then, as the changes we initiated have cascaded and transmuted, we have often responded by withdrawing or retreating, puzzled and sometimes cynical. For instance, as the curriculum reform movement turned before our eyes from Beauty into Beast, revealing its alter ego as a national curriculum fired by national testing, we found it hard to love it enough to want to turn it back again into the Princess we remember. But still more troubling to us was that we found that we mostly lacked the skills, the imagination or the collective moral strength to do so, for we had been oversocialised by academic convention.

Now the changes we initiated have returned to roost and we find ourselves confronting some of the same problems in our institutions that we have seen in schools. As the universities try to manage the consequence of what is generally called economic rationality but the sense of which is better captured for most of us in Malcolm Bradbury's term 'sado-monetarism', we find we are no less able to manage the consequences in our places of work. So when we included the term 'social change' in the title of this book we did so acutely aware that we were not concerned just with looking in at change from the outside. Contemporary academic work is marked by social reconstruction; the reworking of relationships between researchers and subjects, supervisors and students, the organisational structure of the university and other relations which are equally social if less obviously so, between data and interpretation, theory and practice, scholarship and application, assessment and review.

When students turn to us for help in the planning, design, delivery and evaluation of education and training programmes in situations marked by changes that are social, economic, organisational and personal, our first response is that we recognise that we share their problem rather than that we know the solution. The traditional basis of our authority can no longer be sustained by recourse to our roles as those to whom the elders in the tribe have passed the secrets that sustain the culture. If there is a legitimate moral and practical basis for leadership it must lie in our own practice, our reflexivity in relation to it and our ability to communicate it. Our retreat to jargon is cut off, our claims to independence have to be earned and our ability to teach consequent on our own capacity to learn. This is not a problem out of which we can lecture our escape (or even achieve by adopting heavily rhetorical prose or using flowery metaphors in writing books).

BACK TO WORK

Let us return to the students. We have argued that the diversity of experience they bring to the university provides us with a curriculum challenge. If their interest is in developing research skills relevant to their (changing) work then we need to begin by developing a better under-standing of their situation. We asked a group of people just beginning a research methods unit we devised as part of Deakin University's educational doctoral program, to tell us how they encountered research in their daily work, in the broader context of the workplace and about the ways research had been a part of their professional development. Following our own advice, we asked them to use diagrams and drawings to explain these things. Two such diagrams, in which students responded to the question 'How do you see the organisational context in which you plan to do research?', are included here (see Illustrations 14 and 15). They are pro-vided by Sally and Jane. Sally and Jane work in distance education units in two different universities, that is to say, their work involves them in working with academics to produce courses that will be made available to students by printed text or other media. Their role is both a bridging role (between faculty and course producers and to some degree between students and teachers) and one necessarily tied to organisationally set deadlines and objectives. Both Sally and Jane are interested in doing research in case study form as a way of helping them to understand better the detailed working of this complex social context in which they work. Note that we have changed some of the details of their diagrams here to lessen the likelihood of individuals being identifiable.

A number of things struck us about these pictures. First both are very complex, Sally's picture is clearly closely tuned to an appreciation of what she sees to be a very complicated organisation and this reflects her role as a manager of the unit. The university no doubt has organisational plans of its own which show a more straightforward line management and separation of functions. The point is not to criticise the way the university is set up,

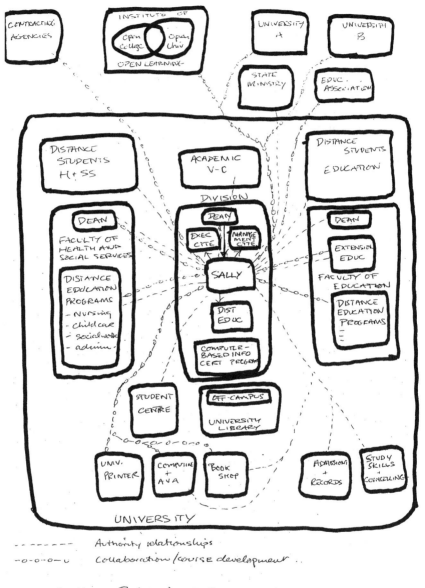

CONTRACTING AGENCIES

INSTITUTE OF
Open College   Open Univ
OPEN LEARNING

UNIVERSITY A

UNIVERSITY B

STATE MINISTRY

EDUC. ASSOCIATION

DISTANCE STUDENTS H+SS

ACADEMIC V-C

DIVISION

DISTANCE STUDENTS EDUCATION

DEAN

FACULTY OF HEALTH AND SOCIAL SERVICES

DISTANCE EDUCATION PROGRAMS
- Nursing
- childcare
- social work
- admin.

DEAN

EXEC CTTE   MANAGEMENT CTTE

SALLY

DIST EDUC

COMPUTER-BASED INFO CERT PROGRAM

DEAN

EXTENSION EDUC

FACULTY OF EDUCATION

DISTANCE EDUCATION PROGRAMS

STUDENT CENTRE

OFF-CAMPUS UNIVERSITY LIBRARY

UNIV. PRINTER

COMPUTING + AVA

BOOK SHOP

ADMISSION + RECORDS

STUDY SKILLS COUNSELLING

UNIVERSITY

- - - - - - -   Authority relationships
-o-o-o-u   Collaboration/course development

Sally : Professional Boundaries

Illustration 14 Sally's workplace: a professional map

but to illustrate the inherent organisational complexity of the situation in which Sally has to work. Part of this complexity comes from the weak separation in her diagram between formal and informal aspects of the situation, a separation that is always implicit in official plans (and always

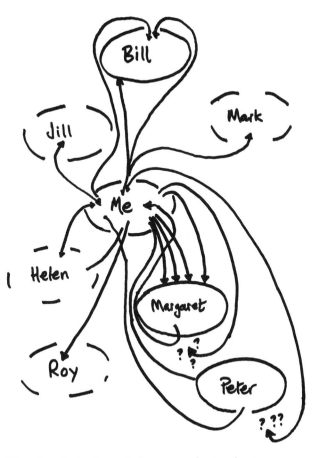

Illustration 15 Jane's workplace: a professional map

so as to make the informal invisible). But the kind of work Sally does is only possible if she is able to make a role for herself (as opposed to taking a role that is fully defined for her), and this means developing relationships with people that stretch beyond what is formally required.

Some of these questions were picked up and developed in an e-mail posting Rob sent to Sally:

> Some people seem very close to you, or at least close in defining for you what counts as useful and valid professional work. Others seem quite distant. [For instance] . . . there are some footsteps in the snow down at the bottom right of the diagram which seem less direct and hurried than (say) the arrow to the Dean.
> . . . If you asked different people to describe what they thought your job was, what do you think they would say? Are those further from your

role more likely to perceive you as the person you are rather than in terms of the responsibilities you have, or is it the other way round? (In some relationships it might be better to be liked than to be thought efficient, in others the opposite!)

. . . One of the questions this raises is about how you do research in positions where power is asymmetrically distributed. (Can you treat everyone as equal when the context is one where they are not?)

(from <rob@deakin.edu.au> 3/9/92)

Jane's picture may look, at first sight, to be less complicated but when she talks about the nature of the relationships depicted here by simple lines and arrows, it is clear that here, too, relationships are complex and the separation of 'formal' and 'informal' is not helpful as a descriptive or explanatory device. Jane works as an instructional designer rather than as a manager, but when she explains her diagram some of the same complexity of relationships implicit in Sally's diagram emerges here too. For instance:

Bill is the Dean, we have a rather formal relationship. I have good access to the Dean, as indicated by the double-arrow path, but our contacts are rare . . . . I will sometimes approach the Dean and his office door is usually open, although he is often booked up with meetings as is indicated by the mostly solid unbroken circle around him. The Dean has definite ideas about the direction in which he would like the Division to head and will support anyone who does things that further his vision. However, he does not always go along with collegial decisions and has been known on several occasions to exercise 'executive privilege' to overturn decisions of the majority of the faculty . . . .

Margaret is the director of the unit. Margaret and I used to have a very open professional relationship; in fact she was a great mentor to me in my early years as a designer. However, as time has gone on, she has let herself become increasingly pressured by academic and administrative demands. She has become more conservative in her approach, possibly because of her position as a full professor . . . . I feel she has either resisted or not supported many of the ideas I have suggested, especially after I achieved tenure. She has also become much cooler and it is very hard to access her as can be seen by the solid line around her and the numerous one-way arrows leading from me to her walls. Because she is the director it is difficult for me to decline her requests, but I am doing so more and more because there is less and less reciprocation. Sometimes I don't know if she will let me discuss things with her as is indicated by the arrow from me to her with question marks. Needless to say, our relationship has become much more formal over the last two years. She is a very careful academic and respected for her work, which is mostly quantitative, but is becoming, in her extremely careful way, increasingly qualitative. I am concerned for her because her life seems to me to be unbalanced. My relationship with Margaret is a definite constraint and one I am unhappy about.

In designing conventional research studies people are not usually considered except as exemplars of roles or clusters of variables. As Rob indicated in his note to Sally, most studies proceed on the assumptions of classical sampling – that is that individuals might be categorised by variables but not as individuals acting and interacting with one another as part of a complex and changing network. Recognition of the validity of the pictures Sally and Jane have drawn (aside from the issue of whether you accept the specific pictures they draw) make it very difficult to proceed to a conventional research design. It might be possible to generate hypotheses that could be tested by looking at a wider range of situations, but it is hard to imagine that the outcome of such a study would offer much that would help understand these situations any better than Jane and Sally (and the people they work with) understand them already. Designing research studies in these circumstances means recognising the politics inherent in the situation, and perhaps more important, recognising that Jane and Sally are themselves a part of the situations that they describe, and so integral with its politics.

Another aspect of these situations which has to be taken into account is their changing character. This isn't easily captured in a diagram but is a feature of the workplace journals that we ask students to write. Consider, for example, these extracts from Mark's journal. Mark works as a training instructor in the navy:

22nd March 1994
The Defence Force Physical Training School are conducting an advanced physical trainers' course. One of the things they want to include on the course is for trainees to give presentations on a variety of topics . . . . Where I have been asked to assist is in developing assessment criteria for the presentations. I would like to try and persuade them to use a self-analysis approach . . . . Place the responsibility on the trainee . . . to provide a descriptive assessment on how it went, if they achieved what they set out to achieve, what if anything they would do differently next time, that sort of thing. Of course the instructors will have to be involved in this process. I have a gut feeling that they are going to prefer a checklist of sorts that they can sit back and tick. I hope I am wrong.

   . . . *At an earlier stage I was talking about letting go. Now I am saying I am comfortable with control. Is this a contradiction? Am I saying one thing but feeling or believing another?*

24th March 1994

It went even better than I expected. I was able to sit down with the three staff from the Physical Training School and together we worked things through. Their concern was that they felt as if the trainees would demand more structure than they were prepared to provide. Just talking through their perceptions and fears was enough for them to sort out their own direction for themselves . . . . At the end of our discussion the senior instructor made two interesting comments back to back. He said, 'These sort of ideas make the job of instructing all that harder. It should have happened twenty years ago!' This would have to be the most positive feedback I've ever received . . . .

On reflection I wonder if I haven't encouraged the Physical Training staff to over-extend themselves. Acknowledging the difficulties I am having with letting go, is it reasonable to encourage others to try it?

Sally, Jane and Mark are engaged in research that is closely related to specific tasks, programmes and organisations. The people with whom they work are critical, for different people in the same roles may react or respond quite differently from one another. The danger in interpreting these situations is metaphorically to line up people on moral criteria (some of them are wrong, or bad and others right, or good). Such polarised views of social processes are often tempting (no less to sociologists and management experts than to the rest of us) but in the end they are not helpful. What we need, as Sally, Jane and Mark show, is an understanding of situations that is sensitive to complexity and questions its own tendencies to simplify.

Often we attempt to account for these complexities by using a term like 'context'. The 'contexts' within which Sally, Jane and Mark work are different, we say, and we intend this to act as a way of explaining all that is puzzling, idiosyncratic or unknown. A recent study by Dorothy Holland and James Reeves (1994) of students being trained as software engineers suggests that other ways of looking at the relationships between people and work might be more useful. In their study they observed three 'teams' of students ('A', 'B' and 'C') who had been trained in a rational approach to the tasks they faced and were then given group projects on which to work over a period of three months. They expected the teams to follow similar approaches, given the nature of the training they had, but this assumed that they would give equal emphasis to the different features of the work. In the event the opposite proved to be the case:

The three teams we chose to follow from their projects' start to finish differed greatly in where and how they planned and carried out tasks such as designing a program, writing code, attending to relations with the boss and client, and preparing user and implementation manuals . . .

despite constant lessons on the rational and business-oriented conduct of programming projects (including demands that the division of labour follow that of commercial software teams), and despite frequent supervision from the teacher (called 'the boss' for the purpose of the projects), the teams managed to organise their activities in ways in which all, to a greater or lesser extent, circumvented class lessons. Team A saw its project as an opportunity to develop an elegant, efficient program; Team B focused instead on satisfying institutional demands in exchange for institutional rewards; and Team C became so enmeshed in internal and external struggles that the relationships among its members frequently became the object of its work.

(Holland and Reeves 1994: 9)

In their discussion of this study Holland and Reeves develop the notion of 'perspective' as a means by which groups attempt to resolve some of the contradictions implicit in any work task within an organisation. Looking to studies of cognition in practice, for instance Jean Lave's (1988) studies of supermarket shoppers and David Middleton's (1987) account of a group of English morris dancers trying to remember a dance, and trying to incorporate this within Marxist notions of alienation and contradiction, they write:

For the case of intellectual labor, 'perspective' highlights and problematizes the relationship between the workers and those who would manage them and/or a system that treats their labor as though it were an abstract entity. 'Perspective' draws attention to the likelihood that workers (or students) construct viewpoints on their projects that are somewhat independent of the viewpoint advocated by their bosses (or teachers), and that these perspectives, even though they are sometimes embedded in practice and scarcely developed discursively, may be the basis from which workers and students react to and sometimes resist institutional attempts at disciplining them. 'Perspective', at the least, is a hedge against over-simplified views of context that adopt ideological, institutionally-given views of the activity at hand, or otherwise ignore the unsettled and conflicted relations of boss to employee, teacher to student, and one team member to another.

(Holland and Reeves 1994: 19)

As an example of the importance of different perspectives to those in the workplace, Team B, the group of students who consistently looked beyond the task at hand to the grading practices of the university, succeeded in gaining high marks for their project even though they succeeded in writing only twelve lines of code in what was intended to be a close simulation of 'real' work!

Although Holland and Reeves do not comment on the fact, it is unlikely to have passed their notice that they too work in organisations within which they have developed 'perspectives' in order to manage the multiple demands on them in their work as academics. Are they like Team A, Team B or Team C? Or are they more like the 'cosmopolitans' described by Alvin Gouldner (1957, 1958) in his study of academic cultures in a College of Education? Sally, Jane and Mark, and you too no doubt, come to the task of doing research from a perspective that is already a part of your role and position within an organisation. This presents a somewhat more complex problem, for the perspective that counts is not one that is temporary, tailored to current fashion and may be discarded (in the way for instance that many ethnographers describe the 'fieldwork role'). As the insider there is no escape from self, your capacity for generating credible fiction (i.e. for lying) or feigning innocence is restricted, indeed once it is known that research is part of the game you are playing you are likely to be closely scrutinised, not to say mocked, by those with whom you work.

The argument we are trying to develop is that, rather than look at the workplace as describing the 'context' within which people work, that is to see 'self' and 'work' as concepts that are identifiably separate from one another, it is better to reconceptualise the person and context as mutually dependent. Therefore it is important to look more closely at how the role of the individual is linked to the overall system of the workplace, which often turns out to be an interwoven net of changing relationships within structural constraints.

Christoph Thomann and Friedemann Schulz von Thun (1988: 22) have offered a model which we find helpful in analysing the playing field (see Figure 6).

They differentiate between the aspects of the individual and the system as well as the aspects of process and structure. Under 'process' they summarise all events which happen in the 'here-and-now' or, looking back to key scenes, in the 'there-and-then'. By 'structure', they refer to the interactional and other processes which have consolidated as personality characteristics and interactional patterns. Using these two concepts, the model they generate offers four 'types' with which to look at workplace situations more closely:

	PROCESS	STRUCTURE
INDIVIDUAL	1	3
SYSTEM	2	4

Figure 6 Reconceptualising the person and the context
Source: Thomann and Schulz von Thun 1988

The *first quadrant* refers to the individual in the here-and-now or in the there-and-then and thus includes most of what we would be likely to include if we were to write a descriptive account of the person's work. But it also goes beyond this to allow the person to ask such questions as, for example, what's actually happening here and now as far as I am concerned? What do I actually want? Or, what led me to act that way then? These questions all relate to what is called '*self-clarification*'.

The *second quadrant*, defined by 'process' and 'system', calls for '*communication clarification*'. Here the key question concerns shared understandings of organisational processes, how can we make things that are clear to us, transparent to others? To take Jane's drawing as an example, would Margaret see things the same way? Has Jane ever tried to share her perceptions with Margaret? Would others in the situation see the relationship between Jane and Margaret much as Jane describes it?

The *third quadrant* lies between the individual and the structural, and working in this area requires '*personality clarification*'. Here we think of questions like, how have I become who I am now? Which are the main traits of my identity? Which personal beliefs are important for me? How do those beliefs relate to the social structure – to race, class and gender, for instance? In Mark's journal we can see the beginnings of this process of questioning.

The *fourth quadrant* deals with those interactional structures of a system which in the course of time have led to certain rules in the actions, and working in this area is known as '*system clarification*'. Here we try to answer questions like, which general structures, routines and schemes have led to the present situation?

We have found this a useful way of avoiding too strong a conceptualisation (and so, separation) in terms of 'person' and 'context' (see Figure 7). Since it indicates the need for different kinds and levels of clarification it avoids too easy use of stereotypes or adopting too quickly the moral categorisations of people which usually form the main themes of office gossip! If, for example, we look at how Sally, Jane and Mark explain relationships on their diagrams we can see how they separate the level of the individual from that of the system and how they locate process within structures rather than seeing this as an opposition.

	PROCESS	STRUCTURE
INDIVIDUAL	self-clarification	personality clarification
SYSTEM	communication clarification	system clarification

Figure 7 Areas of clarification
Source: Thomann and Schulz von Thun 1988

While the model we have just described is usually used in organisational development, it is also useful in designing research, since it incorporates the researcher within the study rather than as an outside agent who is not part of the organisation, its processes, structure and culture. Having to locate yourself on the diagram forces attention on *self-clarification*, for instance on the question, how do I see research and me right now?

It is one thing to find ways to locate oneself but another, often more difficult problem, to find ways to manage one's research agenda in the workplace, a problem demanding *communication clarification*. This, for example, comes clear in Jane's account of her relationship with her director, which has become 'a definite constraint and one I am unhappy about'. She is quite clear about the problems herself, but she feels she cannot communicate them to Margaret, her boss, in a way which might not make them worse. Thinking about a problem like this in terms of the diagram identifies the different ways and different levels in which this relationship might be seen, and so invites the development of alternative, or multiple, strategies for dealing with it. This approach may then suggest ways Jane might attempt to mediate and also ways in which the research might best proceed.

Most relationship problems do not apply only to the here-and-now but have a history, both on the individual and social level. Since 'relationships', in the sense we normally use the term to refer to those with whom we work, are located in the quadrant asking for *personality clarification*, we should deal with this in more detail. Based on Fritz Riemann's foundations of fear (Riemann 1975), Thomann and Schulz von Thun (1988) have suggested four dimensions in human phenomena. This model differentiates four fundamental tendencies, which can be activated intrapersonally and interpersonally:

1 Closeness
   The wish for the familiar, the longing for love and social contact. Harmony and commitment, the need for human contact and social interests, security and tenderness.
2 Distance
   The wish to be different from others in order to be an individual. Freedom, independence and autonomy, the longing for clear realisation of the intellect. This tendency describes those needs of a human being which have to do with always wanting to maintain a certain distance from other people.
3 Continuity
   The longing for continuity and the wish for reliability and order stress other tendencies, which can be described by the following words: planning, precaution, goals, rule and order, theory, power and control. They comprise everything which outlasts the moment in order to gain safety through security.

4 Change

This tendency describes the wish for the magic of the new, the attraction of the unknown and the adventure: living for the spur of the moment and breaking the frame of the ordinary; the longing for spontaneity and passion, highlights and ecstasy, charm and suggestion. These words describe the general need for alternation and change.

It is important, here as before, not to use these categories to stereotype people. The four dimensions are true for most people in some way or other, but in different relations. Everybody has all tendencies to a varying degree and in varying intensity and order. They can become values to individuals and systems and can clash in personal and professional relationships. Perhaps this will be clearer if we reform the diagram, throwing away the boxes and seeing things more in the sense of vectors. These tendencies can be seen as polarities with a crossing and zero point, which form a reticle with four poles running away from the centre (see Figure 8).

Of course this is a model that can be applied, not just in research, but *to* research. It can help in analysing the complex human aspects of the research relationships and can suggest possible development areas. This is particularly important for the micropolitics that always are a part of research, and the macropolitics that always find their way into evaluation.

Thinking back to the previous chapter, this prompts us to say that this model may be most useful within supervision, for it is a good way of thinking about possible directions for a research study and for deciding what the scope of the study should be, that is what questions need to be

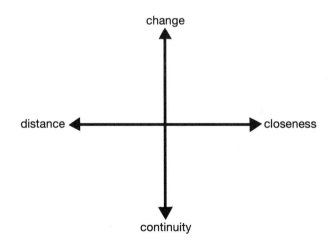

Figure 8 Dimensions of involvement
Source: Thomann and Schulz von Thun 1988

included and what can be left outside the study. It is also, of course, useful for looking at supervision itself where, as we have indicated, it is often very difficult to find the best places to draw lines between what is best treated as clarification of self, of personality, of communication or of the system, for students and supervisors alike.

Look back at Jane's diagram (p. 153), where she describes how her relationship with Margaret 'has become a definite constraint', and one with which she is unhappy. Previously she used to have 'a very open professional relationship'. There used to be a certain closeness and continuity in their work, which can be traced on the respective axis in Figure 8. Meanwhile Jane has achieved tenure and therefore reached a position in which she has developed new ideas, which means from a position of stability she has been able to venture into the quality of the counter-tendency (change). At the same time Margaret 'has become more conservative in her approach, possibly because of her position as a full professor'. Her academic position has brought a lot of attributes to life which we allocated above to the tendency of continuity (e.g. safety, rule and order, theory, power and control). Jane's comment that 'she has also become much cooler and it is very hard to access her' indicates that she has moved more towards the distance pole. On her diagram this dimension of distance and continuity is clearly expressed 'by the solid line around her and the numerous one-way arrows leading from me to her walls . . . . Needless to say, our relationship has become much more formal over the last two years.'

The structure of the relationship between these two actors in the workplace (quadrant three in Figure 6) is superimposed by the interactional structures of the research worlds they adhere to ('quantitative' vs. 'qualitative'). This leads us into quadrant four (*system clarification*), between the system and the social structure, where we asked 'Which general structures, routines and schemes have led to the present situation?'

The importance of these distinctions in the 'real' world of work is that they prompt you to think about problems which have expressed themselves as 'relationship' problems in terms of other levels. Once you have been able to differentiate between these levels you are less likely to try, for instance, to change system structures by personal means alone. This is difficult to do alone and it is an important task for the supervisor, or teacher in research classes, to work out these different aspects and offer support from the position of the outsider. We have been trying to achieve this here by discussing the students' diagrams from various perspectives but there is really no substitute for looking more closely at situations that are close to hand, and in which the researchers are closely involved or implicated. Since our students were not present we had to tape our discussions and send the tapes to their more or less distant learning places. This has had at least one advantage: they can be listened to several times, which our students have

Illustration 16 Living sociogram: Estonia.
This picture shows how Michael applied this method working with heads of schools in Estonia, who are explaining to one another why they have chosen to stand in the positions they have taken.

always found very useful and sometimes have used as a key point of reference for them in their work.

Working with people who are researching in their own work(place), we have explored different ways in which the notions of continuity and change, closeness and distance, which play a vital part in how research actually confronts the agents with each other, can be put into practice. The most successful method we know is one we learnt from Wilfried Schley from the University of Zurich. This gives a very vivid view of the social structure

Illustration 17 Thinking about change and continuity: Croatia

within an organisation by involving participants directly and it is an approach we have found useful in workshops and in-service programmes. To run it, we use index cards to mark the four poles (Figure 8) on the floor and then form the reticle by combining them horizontally and vertically with masking tape. Note that the poles should be distant enough from each other for a group of people to stand in each quadrant, depending on the size of the group. Everyone is then asked to locate themselves on the diagram and stand on this spot within the diagram on the floor. The group thus forms a living sociogram (often quite a dynamic one as people jostle for space, which in itself can become an important point for discussion!) (see Illustrations 16 and 17).

9 Windows to look through/windows to break, open or close

And now, having brought this fiction to a thoroughly traditional ending, I had better explain that although all that I described in the last two chapters happened, it did not happen quite in the way you may have been led to believe.

(John Fowles, *The French Lieutenant's Woman*)

In his novel *The French Lieutenant's Woman* John Fowles presents a compelling narrative in the style of a romantic historical novel and then, at the climax of the story, unexpectedly offers 'alternative' endings. The novel has as one of its themes the consequences for interpersonal relationships of social and intellectual changes in mid-nineteenth-century England and this disruption, in what first presents itself as a conventional text, signals to the reader a quantum jump in the human imagination more effectively than any amount of explanation. On a more modest scale, in this chapter we are looking for a way to unite the different ways we have represented, and responded to, current changes in the small world of social research; changes that also have consequences for the character of sensibility.

In the narrative structure of this enquiry our need is not for different endings so much as for multiple entries. The grand narratives normally implicit in research methodology textbooks rarely allow the space to ask, who is doing research on whom, for whom and why? Still less do they falter in their confidence in the moral purpose of research, which is normally taken to be self-evident. But as the universities come closer to government and the interests of the state, as the research process folds in and back on itself in many complex ways, and as research becomes, to some degree, everyone's business, such questions become increasingly troubling. So, we will conclude, not by offering closure but by drawing on some more general assumptions which underlie the individual chapters of the book to try to see new ways forward.

We begin with the abstract of one of the courses we teach, where we attempt to confront our students with the philosophy and methodology of our approach:

In the last twenty years, as the social sciences themselves have changed, there has been a marked shift in research in education away from large scale surveys, testing programs and experimental psychology toward studies that are small scale, low tech and case based. Instead of emphasising measurement much educational research now mostly uses descriptive methods. Where once the concern was with scientific method and generalisation, research now looks more to political considerations, to local change and to understanding issues.

In this seminar we will take some of these ideas and test them in the context of the interest in peace and peace education that people bring to the seminar. What we will be looking for is finding ways to build a capacity for research into the work that people do rather than adding research as a specialist set of skills. We will use a variety of methods for doing this, involving you in various research exercises and role plays as well as more formal discussion.

We will introduce Readings as we go and allow you time to read and discuss these. We will also expect you to write regularly! Assignments will be negotiated with students. Group and collaborative assignments are encouraged.

(European Peace University Prospectus 1994)

After the first couple of days, having tried some of the research exercises we have described in this book, some students came to us to ask, 'Tell us now exactly what you're up to!' This reminds us (and the example is not an isolated case) how difficult it is to break from the authority structures that conventionally define teaching (and learning). It brings us too to a question that lies at the heart of this book, for we have tried in our teaching/writing to bring together the act, the process, of teaching/writing and what we are teaching/writing *about*, for this seems to be an intention that lies at the heart of what it means to be reflexive (Ashmore 1989). The question is further complicated by the fact that research too is both intention and action, process and content, yet it is difficult to find a way round the assumption that research must be 'on' education rather than 'in' education, as though these were quite separate concerns.

The problem we have just described has been continually accompanying us while writing this book, from finding an appropriate title to giving it an ending that says what we want it to say. How, we constantly ask ourselves, can educational research itself be educational? Our uncertainties may be characteristic of the present time, in which social change is everywhere, even in educational research as it has diversified and elaborated its methods and interacted with changes taking place in the social sciences and in cultural studies. The only consistency is in change itself: πάντα ρεῖ. This notion is threatening because it takes away the feeling that there is stability, continuity and a sense of security to be found in method – in the routine use of standard research tools which can be relied upon to tell us 'how things are for sure'.

We would like to be able to answer the question the students asked us simply and directly, but the question itself is more demanding than it might seem, for even to acknowledge it is to undo the logic of the curriculum we intended. Yet we know too that not to try and answer in a simple and direct way is to reinforce the suspicion that we are merely playing a game based only on the teacher's power and the student's dependence. The best we can do in the situation is to attempt to displace the question. We evaluate the course, not on the answers students are able to give at the end, but by the nature of the new questions that they ask themselves but cannot answer.

WHAT IS WRONG WITH QUALITATIVE RESEARCH?

In the late 1960s, as educational research began to look at the possibilities and potential for qualitative research against a background of a research tradition dominated by testing and survey research, there was the unstated promise that such a shift in methods might help resolve some of these questions. It was a faith that proved to be misplaced, for as qualitative research has become more accepted, so it has taken on some of the exclusiveness of all established academic knowledge. The shift to the use of a wider spectrum of research methods in the last twenty years has led to new questions and new topics as well as to new ways of doing research, but it has not made research any more accessible, more widely used or more democratic. At the present time, educational researchers can turn in almost any direction to draw on qualitative research models that can be used to study education in ways that make their work publicly more accessible. They can, but for the most part they do not.

The overwhelming impression we have from attending meetings like the American Educational Research Association annual meeting, keeping a weather eye on academic journals, reading student dissertations and papers and looking at courses in research methods in universities is that while there is still energy and enthusiasm for qualitative research, a new orthodoxy threatens to emerge. In education, and also in sociology, social work, nursing and other areas, qualitative research is now the dominant form of research in many universities; sometimes it is the only form. As qualitative research, in all its various forms, becomes part of the mainstream, we are beginning to see new problems emerging:

- Often, it seems, qualitative methods are adopted within what is still essentially a quantitative (or at least an empiricist) paradigm. The nature of the data changes but the research methods remain much the same. Theory and interpretation are separated from data collection; the objectivity of the researcher is managed by adopting standard procedures; the voice of the researcher is the voice-over of an apparently unimplicated narrator.

- Studies that are descriptive do offer a real opportunity for research to extend its democratic reach. But while case studies provide a possibility to extend the informed audience for research, in practice much of what is written is impenetrable, self-referential, confusing and exclusive. The registers and tropes of the written language of research have replaced statistics in ensuring that few readers have the specialised literary competence to participate in discussions about research (as this sentence alone demonstrates).

- Some see in case study a requirement to create large amounts of descriptive data but they resist the opportunity to theorise. The result is often that studies and reports are filled with slabs of lightly edited transcript which are organised into ad hoc categories but there is little questioning or demonstrated understanding of the problem of making it mean something. Often, it seems, we refer to 'grounded theory' as a reference point, but use it to produce all ground and no theory.

- Many of us turn to action research, seeing in it a solution to the problem of managing our own convictions while conducting credible and legitimate research within the arena of our own circumstances. Two distinct dangers await us! One is the temptation to sidestep the threat inherent in all action research by reconceptualising it as something that others will do, so putting us in the safe role of facilitators or promoters of action research. The other is that once we get started we fall back into the conventional paradigm. We may review the literature well enough, but then lose our way, again find ourselves overwhelmed by quantities of data, and fail to develop incisive and strategic action plans. We end up with research that is about action, but not action research.

- While many new methodological labels abound, if you skip the introduction and go straight to the evidence and its interpretation, it is not always easy to see what makes studies that present themselves as post-structural or post-modern (for instance) distinctive. In many cases the methods and the data look very similar.

- We adopt models ('interpretive', 'socially critical', 'democratic', 'responsive', for example) that appear to fit our research needs but then we fail to act consistently. For instance, few socially critical studies are critical of themselves, not many responsive studies respond, many democratic evaluations are autocratic and not many interpretive studies attempt to interpret the interpreter. *Mea culpa.*

In this book we have tried to break a mould that was in a small way of our own making. We have placed change at the centre of this book because it connects our other principal themes, the need critically to reinstate subjectivity in the face of a decline in confidence in objectivity, the individuality of individual and society and the socially constructed nature of perception, self and action. The topics, themes and concerns of action learning, process management and action research, particularly what Robin McTaggart, Stephen Kemmis, Colin Henry, Orlando Fals-Borda and others call 'participatory action research', so as to distinguish it from forms of action research adopted as an instrument of policy by commercial and government bureaucracies, provide a constant sub-text in this book (see, for instance, McTaggart 1991, Carr and Kemmis 1986, Henry 1992, Fals-Borda and Rahman 1991). Action research attracts considerable attention because it appears to offer a way to regain control over changes that we feel are running beyond our capacity to control them, and particularly those changes that stem from the authority of the state. In this sense it is, as Stephen Kemmis points out, an essentially modernist response to the threat of post-modernity, a reassertion of liberal humanism in the face of new forms of authority, forms which have stimulated the intellectual crises posed by the authorless text, the emergence of global capitalism and the end of history (Kemmis 1992).

What often seems to be at stake in action research is a contest between alternative notions of democracy. In many action research studies the dominant narrative is that of the 'participatory' democracy of grass-roots initiated reform testing the will and commitment of 'representative' democracy, as this is expressed through the actions of those in large-scale bureaucracies. Often it seems as though the first sees the second as the ruthless exercise of hierarchical authority, while it itself is seen as representing only sectional self-interest. Consequently, reduced to two-dimensional images of the social world, many advocates of action research lapse into presenting themselves in heroic roles.

John Elliott, recognising that professionals can no longer sustain a façade of disinterest, sees the need for educational action research to find a way of escape from this cul-de-sac by breaking the consensus created by constructing situations in terms of inflexible opposing views. He proposes a reconstitution of action research around the plurality of educational interests participating in a particular case, rather than continuing to see it as the cutting tool of radical groups or justified solely in terms of professional interest. Taking his key assumptions we arrive at four 'understandings' of the problems of educational change. We have generalised these from their original form as statements about teaching, schools and classrooms so that they may be applied in other settings.

- Individuals cannot significantly improve their practice in isolation without opportunities for discussion with significant others.
- Attempts to change practice by changing organisations and organisa-

tional systems through hierarchically initiated and controlled reforms will be resisted and are likely to fail.

- Neither administratively-led organisational reviews nor privatised self-reflection on the part of individuals are likely to make any significant impact on the quality of practice.
- The institutionalisation of an effective process of evaluation can be facilitated or frustrated by middle management or external agents, but it can only be realised through the free association of individuals networking across the system to study their own practices.

(Adapted from Elliott 1993: 176)

These statements present us with a new problem, and it is a problem we recognise since it frequently arises when research confronts action. Rational, clear and incisive as they are, once these statements (or others of a similar character) are carried into practice a new set of problems arises. At their centre is what often happens when 'individuals', 'organisations' and 'others' interact and someone tries to introduce change. Most of this book has been taken up with explorations of this one sentence, but for the moment we can summarise what we see as the nature of the problem when individuals, organisations and others face change:

- Any change generates information, both immediately and as fall-out; or as sociologists would say, both formal and informal.
- Information will travel through a system at different speeds, some having a longer half-life than others. Most importantly, information will mutate as it passes from one person to another and it will do so in unpredictable ways. For managers to issue written statements in an attempt to clarify matters will exacerbate the problem because any written statement will hide as much, or more, than it reveals, especially in respect of imputed motives. Change in any organisation will exemplify the problem of 'Chinese whispers'.
- Each person will perceive information differently according to their location relative to others, how and when they receive information and what they try to do with it. The more people talk about their different perceptions, the more acute the problem will become, since (as in describing an elephant) their tacit knowledge will always undermine public knowledge.
- Over time, remembered shared events create the basis of an organisational culture. In most organisations it seems that the present pattern is for people in management (and especially senior management) positions to change jobs more often than others. This means that those with the power to make changes are usually outside the culture they wish to change and so do not understand it (cf. Chapter 8).

For these reasons we believe that the ideas raised in this book cannot become part of practice unless we are prepared to incorporate them at different levels of understanding. We can best explain this using the model which we present as an iceberg in Figure 9.

What we see above the imaginary water line is what we normally encounter when people interact. Observing them, and perhaps participating in the situation ourselves, we are aware, from the way they discuss and deliberate, that they are faced with choices, choices which may be limited by their competence but which are expressed as actions and proposals. As we get closer to the metaphoric waterline, we become aware of other forces at work in the situation. 'Judgement' is a feature of the situation that is very difficult to see, and beliefs and values more so. Identity we see only as personality, we don't normally see the person in the sense that we used the term in Chapter 3.

The diagram suggests that we can usually manage change without looking below the waterline by working to develop competence, behaviour and action as they are depicted here. For instance, by choosing to act in different ways we can make changes in what we do in response to changes in our environment. This adaptation will eventually be reflected in our competence. Part of the problem we face seems to be that while we recognise that change extends into hidden areas of the self, for us to venture there always seems like a threat to privacy, an invasion of the self, which is not only unwarranted but perhaps dangerous.

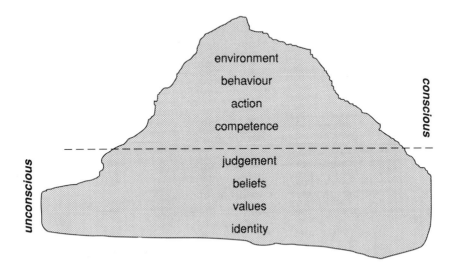

Figure 9 Levels of response to change

Whereas the visible parts of the iceberg are usually recognisably part of the research discourse (as we encounter it in conferences, the research literature, textbooks, etc.), the hidden parts of the iceberg belong to the tacit knowledge of the insiders, forming the 'songlines' of the particular culture. Since it is in this invisible part of ourselves where change must take place, it is important that we find ways of doing research that touch it. This is not to argue that only these hidden parts matter, or that recourse to therapy can give us real answers, for to do so is to recreate the very frame we seek to open. The challenge to research is to find new ways of talking about behaviour *and* motivation, competence *and* judgement, action *and* values, emotion *and* thought, theory *and* practice, not as dualities but as inextricably a part of each other. We need, for instance, to recognise that motivation is an element of behaviour, not a cause of it, that competence cannot be separated from judgement, that thought is an emotion not apart from it, that action is inseparable from belief, and that theory is implicit in practice. And all this, we have consistently argued, cannot be managed individually or in isolation. It requires a collaborative effort and a reassessment of the nature of self in relation to social context, not a submerging of the individual within the collective but a recognition that the person only exists in the light of significant others.

While this last paragraph summarises the best answer we are able to give to the students who asked us, 'But what are you really up to?', it is clear that it is an answer that leaves much unresolved. Undoing two thousand years or so of Western philosophy is going to take more than one conversation (or one book). But we can start.

A device we have found useful as a way of disrupting some of the categories of thought marked by the waterline on the iceberg is the 'Johari window' (Luft 1963). This 'window' is an heuristic instrument which allows you to open the doors of perception on the different areas of shared and private knowledge invoked when people interact (see Figure 10).

The four quadrants in the window can be described as follows:

Area I: the area of *free activity*
This is the area in which people consciously interact, discuss and interpret interactions with one another.

Area II: the area of the *blind spot*
This is the area where others see things about you that you do not recognise yourself. Occasionally you will encounter interpretations made of your actions by others and be surprised if they fall in this area. Those in close groups, like families, may encounter such insights with particular intensity.

	known to oneself	not known to oneself
known to others	I area of free activity	II area of the blind spot
not known to others	III area of avoidance and concealment	IV area of the unknown activity

Figure 10 The Johari window
Source: Luft 1963

Area III: the area of *avoidance and concealment*
This is the area in which you seek to protect your privacy and includes thoughts and desires as well as perceptions of others.

Area IV: the area of *the unknown activity*
This can be a disturbing area to enter and normally we are well able to steer around it, but in times of change you may be drawn in regardless and find much of what you took for granted, in routines and relationships, has changed.

We described the Johari window as having four 'quadrants', but this is not strictly true. The angles of view offered by each part of the window are not equal or equivalent but are more like a selection of lenses you might attach to a camera. Through each window we see different things and we can alter the view by getting closer, polishing areas that may be smudged or opaque. Without over-elaborating the metaphor, the important point to make is that the frames of the window are not fixed, nor are we condemned to be passive observers. Indeed the 'frame', a concept often taken to imply fixed points of reference, may invite a violent response, as we saw in the opening pages of this book. So too with the Johari window, which should not be seen as a picturesque way of framing the view, but as representing frames of knowledge held in place by circumstance, custom and vested interest. The window is there to be challenged, stretched and, sometimes, broken, and of course a frame can itself be a question. Even what seems a straightforward and simple question, like 'What is an elephant?', we have seen can turn back on itself in complex ways when we ask it in a social situation.

Early in this chapter we said that our response to those students who asked us what we were up to was to try and shift the discourse from one marked by simple questions and answers to the replacement of their first questions by more complex ones. Stated in such an abstract way this might seem a classic academic avoidance strategy, and perhaps one that is located in our blind spot! But to end we want to return to the outline we provided for the peace research course and give one student's response to this invitation to struggle with questions the course raised. If this echoes your response to this book we will have achieved all we hoped in writing it, for while Boonda does not mention change explicitly, change is surely in the air:

> It has been an experience I am trying to hold on to as I intuit that there is much more that can be built upon the foundations we were provided with in class. The exercises and themes we touched upon and delved into have shone some light on ways in which I can open the space linking my own opinions, insights, experiences, etc. and that of what I learn and have obtained from other sources. For me it creates a process and means for communicating between theory and praxis.
>
> The motivation for using the exercises to communicate 'simplicity in the complex' or vice-versa and practice applying different forms of representation such as metaphors in explicating things that are conceptually dense is based on the idea that 'unless you are able to create a shared memory for people, they lose what they have learned'.
>
> To this I add the strong belief that theory should come out of 'practice' or at least, theory should reflect the experiences of people, and not exist in itself; an abstracted representation of a universal truth that is ahistorical and without context.
>
> (Boonda Kearns, July 1994)

References

Agar, M. H. (1980) *The Professional Stranger. An informal introduction to ethnography*, New York and Texas: Academic Press.

Albury, R. (1983) *The Politics of Objectivity*, Geelong, Victoria: Deakin University Press.

Ashmore, M. (1989) *The Reflexive Thesis: Wrighting sociology of scientific knowledge*, Chicago: The University of Chicago Press.

Bar-On, D. (1991) 'Trying to understand what one is afraid to learn', in D. Schön (ed.) *The Reflective Turn: Case studies in and on educational practice*, New York: Teachers College Press, 321–42.

Barnes, T. J. and Duncan, J. S. (1992) *Writing Worlds: Discourse, text and metaphor in the representation of landscape*, London: Routledge.

Barthes, R. (1977) *Image – Music – Text*, Glasgow: Fontana.

Barthes, R. (1982) 'The photographic message', in S. Sontag (ed.) *A Barthes Reader*, London: Jonathan Cape, 196–210.

Becher, T. (1989) *Academic Tribes and Territories. Intellectual enquiry and the cultures of disciplines*, Milton Keynes: Open University Press.

Beisser, A. R. (1971) 'The paradoxical theory of change', in J. Forgan and I. L. Shepherd (eds) *Gestalt Therapy Now*, New York: Harper & Row, 77–80.

Berger, J. and Mohr, J. (1982) *Another Way of Telling*, London: Writers and Readers.

Bohm, D. (1965) *The Special Theory of Relativity*, New York: W. A. Benjamin.

Bohm, D. (1985) *Unfolding Meaning: A weekend of dialogue with David Bohm*, edited by Donald Factor, Mickleton, Gloucestershire: Foundation House Publications.

Bovill, M. (1990) *Basic Skills: Numeracy*, London: Broadcasting Research Department, Special Projects, British Broadcasting Corporation.

Bradbury, M. (1993a) *Mensonge*, Harmondsworth: Penguin.

Bradbury, M. (1993b) *Doctor Criminale*, Harmondsworth: Penguin.

Brand, S. (1987) *The Media Lab: Inventing the future at MIT*, New York and Harmondsworth: Viking Penguin.

Carr, W. and Kemmis, S. (1986) *Becoming Critical: Education, knowledge and action research*, London: Falmer Press.

Cazden, C. B. (1988) *Classroom Discourse. The language of teaching and learning*, Portsmouth, NH: Heinemann.

Chaplin, E. (1994) *Sociology and Visual Representation*, London and New York: Routledge.

Clifford, J. and Marcus, G. E. (1986) *Writing Culture: The poetics and politics of ethnography*, Berkeley: University of California Press.

Collier, J. (1967) *Visual Anthropology: Photography as a research method*, New York: Holt, Rinehart & Winston.

Collins, A. (1991) *'Jugs and Herrings': Children's perceptions of the world of drugs*, Geelong, Victoria: Deakin Institute for Studies in Education.

Connell, R. W. (1985) 'How to supervise a PhD', *Vestes*, 2: 38–41.

Cooper, H. M. (1989) *Integrating Research. A guide for literature reviews*, Newbury Park and London: Sage.

Crawford, J., Kippax, S., Onyx, J., Gault, U. and Benton, P. (1992) *Emotion and Gender*, London: Sage.

Davis, J. (1992) 'Tense in ethnography: some practical considerations', in J. Okely and H. Callaway (eds) *Anthropology and Autobiography*, London: Routledge, 205–20.

Deakin University (1994) *Unit EAE 411: 'Changing Classrooms'*, Geelong, Victoria: Deakin University Press.

Devereux, G. (1973) *Angst und Methode in den Verhaltenswissenschaften*, Frankfurt/M.: Suhrkamp.

Eco, U. (1988) *Wie man eine wissenschaftliche Arbeit verfaßt*, Heidelberg: Quelle & Meyer.

Edwards, D. and Mercer, N. M. (1987) *Common Knowledge: The development of understanding in the classroom*, London: Methuen.

Elliott, J. (1993) 'What have we learned from action research in school-based evaluation?', *Educational Action Research*, 1, 1: 175–86.

Ende, M. (1973) *Momo*, Vienna: Verlag Gustav Swoboda & Bruder.

Fabian, J. (1988) Introduction to 'Twenty Years of Critical Anthropology' Conference, Amsterdam.

Fals-Borda, O. and Rahman, M. A. (1991) *Action and Knowledge. Breaking the monopoly with participatory action-research*, New York: Apex Press.

Fay, B. (1977) 'How people change themselves: the relationship between critical theory and its audience', in T. Ball (ed.) *Political Theory and Praxis: New perspectives*, Minneapolis: University of Minnesota Press, 200–33, 266–9.

Ferguson, W. (1993) 'Aesopic Teaching', unpublished paper, Evanston, IL: Northwestern University.

Festinger, L., Reicken, H. W. and Schachter, S. (1964) *When Prophecy Fails: A social and psychological study of a modern group that predicted the destruction of the world*, New York: Harper.

Fineman, S. (ed.) (1993) *Emotion in Organisations*, London: Sage.

Fitzclarence, L. (1991a) 'Mattering maps' internal project document, ARC 'Schooling the Future Project', Faculty of Education, Deakin University, Victoria, Australia.

Fitzclarence, L. (1991b) 'Remembering the reconceptualist project', paper presented at the Bergamo Conference, Dayton, Ohio, 16–19 October.

Fletcher, C. (1975) *The Person in the Sight of Sociology*, London: Routledge & Kegan Paul.

Foucault, M. (1984) *The Foucault Reader*, P. Rabinow (ed.), New York: Pantheon.

Freire, P. (1972) *Pedagogy of the Oppressed*, Harmondsworth: Penguin.

Fuchs, G. and Schratz, M. (eds) (1994) *Interkulturelles Zusammenleben – aber wie? Auseinandersetzung mit alltäglichem und institutionalisiertem Rassismus*, Innsbruck: Österreichischer StudienVerlag.

Geertz, C. (1983) *Local Knowledge*, New York: Basic Books.

Geertz, C. (1988) *Works and Lives: The anthropologist as author*, Cambridge: Polity Press.

Giroux, H. (1992) *Border Crossings: Cultural workers and the politics of education*, New York and London: Routledge.

Goodenough, W. (1965) 'Rethinking "status" and "role": Towards a general model of the cultural organisation of social relationships', in ASA Monographs No. 1, *The Relevance of Models for Social Anthropology*, London: Tavistock.

Gouldner, A. (1957) 'Cosmopolitans and locals: towards an analysis of latent social roles I', *Administrative Science Quarterly*, 2: 281–306.

Gouldner, A. (1958) 'Cosmopolitans and locals: towards an analysis of latent social roles II', *Administrative Science Quarterly*, 3: 444–80.

Groundwater-Smith, S. (1990) *Perspectives on Schools Broadcasting*, Sydney: Curriculum Support Unit, NSW Department of School Education.

Hamilton, D. (1989) *Towards a Theory of Schooling*, Lewes: Falmer.

Hammersley, M. (1983) 'The researcher exposed: a natural history', in R. G. Burgess (ed.) *The Research Process in Educational Settings*, Lewes: Falmer.

Hammersley, M. and Atkinson, P. (1983) *Ethnography: Principles and practice*, London: Tavistock.

Handal, G. and Lauvås, P. (1987) *Promoting Reflective Teaching: Supervision in practice*, Milton Keynes: Open University Press.

Haug, F. (ed.) (1990) *Erinnerungsarbeit*, Berlin: Argument.

Haug, F. *et al.* (1983) *Frauenformen 2: Sexualisierung*, Berlin: Argument.

Haug, F. *et al.* (1987) *Female Sexualisation: A collective work of memory*, London: Verso.

Henry, C. (1992) 'The human face of critical social science: Orlando Fals-Borda and the praxis of participatory action research', Second World Congress on Action Learning, Brisbane, Australia, 14–17 June.

Hentig, H. v. (1985) *Aufgeräumte Erfahrung*, Frankfurt/M.: Ullstein.

Holland, D. and Reeves, J. R. (1994) 'Activity theory and the view from somewhere: team perspectives on the intellectual work of programming', *Mind, Culture and Activity* 1, 1: 8–24.

Jäger, S. (1992) *BrandSätze: Rassismus im Alltag*, Duisburg: Duisburger Institut für Sprach-und Sozialforschung.

Kamler, B., Schratz, M. and Walker, R. (1992) 'Writing a critical review of the research literature'. Audiotape available from the Graduate School of Education, Deakin University, Victoria 3217, Australia. Price A$ 20.

Kemmis, S. (1992) 'Postmodernism and educational research', Seminar on Methodology and Epistemology in Educational Research, University of Liverpool, 22–24 June.

Kippax, S., Crawford, J., Waldby, C. and Benton, P. (1990) 'Women negotiating heterosex: implications for AIDS prevention', *Women's Studies International Forum*, 13, 2: 533–42.

Kounin, J. (1970) *Discipline and Group Management in Classrooms*, New York: Holt, Rinehart & Winston.

Lather, P. (1991) *Getting Smart. Feminist research and pedagogy with/in the postmodern*, New York: Routledge.

Latour, B. (1987) *Science in Action*, Cambridge, Mass.: Harvard University Press.

Lave, J. (1988) *Cognition in Practice. Mind, mathematics and culture in everyday life*, Cambridge: Cambridge University Press.

Li, X. and Crane, N. B. (1993) *Electronic Style: A guide to citing electronic information*, Westport, CT: Meckler.

Lodge, D. (1989) *Nice Work*, Harmondsworth: Penguin.

Logan, T. (1984) in J. Shostak and T. Logan (eds) *Pupil Experience*, London: Croom Helm.

Luft, J. (1963) *Group Processes: An introduction to group dynamics*, Palo Alto: The National Press.

Lurie, A. (1967) *Imaginary Friends*, New York: Avon Books.

Lynn, J. and Jay, A. (1981) *The Complete 'Yes Minister'*, London: BBC Books.

MacDonald, B. and Walker, R. (eds) (1974) *SAFARI 1: Information, evaluation, research and the problem of control*, Norwich: University of East Anglia.

McTaggart, R. (1991) *Action Research: A short modern history*, Geelong, Victoria: Deakin University Press.

Mehan, H. (1979) *Learning Lessons*, Cambridge, Mass.: Harvard University Press.

Meyer, W. (1981) 'Der Gipfel der Gläubigkeit', *Die Zeit*, 36, 45 (30 October): 34.

Middleton, D. (1987) 'Dance to the Music: Conversational remembering and joint activity in learning an English morris dance', *The Quarterly Newsletter of the Laboratory of Comparative Human Cognition*, 9, 1: 23–38.

Miles, R. (1989) *Racism*, London: Routledge.

Norman, D. A. (1988) *The Psychology of Everyday Things*, New York: Basic Books.

Norris, N. (ed.) (1977) *SAFARI: Theory in practice*, Norwich: University of East Anglia.

Oakley, A. (1993) *The Secret Lives of Eleanor Jenkinson*, London: Flamingo.

Okely, J. and Callaway, H. (eds) (1992) *Anthropology and Autobiography*, London: Routledge.

Palmer, P. (1986) *The Lively Audience: A study of children around the TV set*, Sydney: Allen & Unwin.

Pirie, D. P. (1985) *How to Write Critical Essays*, London and New York: Routledge.

Plummer, G., Newman, K. and Winter, R. (1993) 'Exchanging letters: a format for collaborative action research?', *Educational Action Research*, 1, 2: 305–14.

Popkewitz, T. S. (1984) *Paradigm and Ideology in Educational Research. The social functions of the intellectual*, London: Falmer.

Popkewitz, T. S. (1991) *A Political Sociology of Educational Reform. Power/knowledge in teaching, teacher education, and research*, New York: Teachers College Press.

Postman, N. (1993) *Technopoly: The surrender of culture to technology*, New York: Vintage Books.

Powdermaker, H. (1967) *Stranger and Friend: The way of an anthropologist*, New York: W. W. Norton & Co.

Projekt Frauengrundstudium (ed.) (1982) *Frauen-Grundstudium 2*, Berlin: Argument.

Reyem, W. (1980) *Dispensorische Theorie und kritische Gesellschaft*, Oldenburg.

Riemann, F. (1975) *Grundformen der Angst. Eine tiefenpsychologische Studie*, München: Reinhardt.

Sanger, J. (1993) 'Five Easy Pieces: the deconstruction of illuminatory data in research writing', unpublished paper, Norwich: Anglia Polytechnic University.

Saxe, J. G. (1930) *The Victorian Readers: Third book*, Melbourne: H. J. Green.

Schiek, G. (1992) *Eine sozialwissenschaftliche Arbeit schreiben: Praxis, Dialoge, Zwänge*, Baltmannsweiler: Schneider.

Schneider, U. (1988) 'Studienreflexion in Tagebuchform als Prüfungsmethode', in F. Klug and M. Schratz (eds) *Hochschulunterricht unter der Lupe. Projekte und Fallstudien aus der Werkstätte forschenden Lehrens an der Universität Innsbruck*, Innsbruck: Institut für Erziehungswissenschaften, 80–8.

Schratz, M. (1992) 'Rein ins Kalte Wasser? Betreuungsarbeit ist auch Beziehungsklärung', in M. Schratz and S. Steixner (eds) *Betreuung wissenschaftlicher Abschlußarbeiten: Forschen im Dialog*, Innsbruck: Österreichischer StudienVerlag, 75–95.

Schratz, M. and Mehan, H. (1993) 'Gulliver Travels into a Math Class. In search of alternative discourse in teaching and learning', *International Journal of Educational Research*, 19, 3: 247–64.

Sears, J. (1992) 'Researching the other/searching for self: qualitative research on [homo]sexuality in education', *Theory into Practice*, 31, 2: 147–56.

Simons, H. (1987) *Getting to Know Schools in a Democracy*, Lewes: Falmer.

Sinclair, J. McH. and Coulthard, R. M. (1975) *Towards an Analysis of Discourse. The English used by teachers and pupils*, London: Oxford University Press.

Smith Bowen, E. (1954) *Return to Laughter*, New York: Doubleday Anchor.

Sontag, S. (1979) *On Photography*, Harmondsworth: Penguin.

Sparkes, A. (1994) 'Life histories and the issue of voice: reflections on an emerging relationship', *International Journal of Qualitative Studies in Education*, 7, 2: 165–83.

Spindler, G. (ed.) (1988) *Doing the Ethnography of Schooling: Educational anthropology in action*, Prospect Heights, IL: Waveland Press.

Thomann, C. and Schulz von Thun, F. (1988) *Klärungshilfe. Handbuch für Therapeuten, Gesprächshelfer und Moderatoren in schwierigen Gesprächen*, Reinbek: Rowohlt.

Virilio, P. (1989) 'The Museum of Accidents', Toronto: Public Access Collective.

Virilio, P. (1993) 'The Listening Room', Radio broadcast, Sydney: ABC Radio National.

Wax, R. (1971) *Doing Fieldwork: Warnings and advice*, Chicago: University of Chicago Press.

Weedon, C. (1987) *Feminist Practice and Poststructuralist Theory*, Oxford: Basil Blackwell.

Wolf, N. (1990) *The Beauty Myth*, London: Vintage.

Woodward, F. L. (transl.) (1985) *The Minor Anthologies of the Pali Canon*, Part 2, London: The Pali Text Society (Routledge).

Index